AMERICAN
HERITAGE

February 1961 · Volume XII, Number 2

For all our progress in other areas, allegory has taken a nose dive since 1800, the year when this mourning piece by John Coles, Jr., was probably engraved. Where would you find today such a satisfying jumble of symbols—cannons, cupids, angels, goddesses of wisdom and patriotism, torches, garlands, liberty caps, a blubbering soldiery? Even the "Senate" membership is a purely classical allusion.

AMERICAN HERITAGE

The Magazine of History

PUBLISHER
James Parton

EDITORIAL DIRECTOR
Joseph J. Thorndike, Jr.

SENIOR EDITOR
Bruce Catton

EDITOR
Oliver Jensen

MANAGING EDITOR
Eric Larrabee

ASSOCIATE EDITORS
Richard M. Ketchum
Joan Paterson Mills
Robert L. Reynolds

ASSISTANT EDITORS
Helen M. Brown, Robert Cowley
Stephen W. Sears

LIBRARIAN
Caroline Backlund

COPY EDITOR
Beverly Hill

ASSISTANT: Naomi S. Weber

ART DIRECTOR
Irwin Glusker

ASSOCIATE ART DIRECTOR: Murray Belsky
STAFF PHOTOGRAPHER: Herbert Loebel

ADVISORY BOARD
Allan Nevins, *Chairman*

Ray A. Billington   Alvin M. Josephy, Jr.
Carl Carmer   Richard P. McCormick
Albert B. Corey   Harry Shaw Newman
Christopher Crittenden   Howard H. Peckham
Marshall B. Davidson   S. K. Stevens
Louis C. Jones   Arthur M. Schlesinger, Sr.

CIRCULATION DIRECTOR
Richard V. Benson

AMERICAN HERITAGE is published every two
months by American Heritage Publishing Co.,
Inc., 551 Fifth Avenue, New York 17, N. Y.
Single Copies: $3.95
Annual Subscriptions: $15.00 in U.S. & Canada
$16.00 elsewhere

An annual Index of AMERICAN HERITAGE is
published every February, priced at $1.00. A
five-year Cumulative Index of Volumes VI–X
is available at $3.00.

AMERICAN HERITAGE will consider but assumes
no responsibility for unsolicited material.

Title registered U.S. Patent Office.
Second class postage paid at New York, N. Y.

Sponsored by

American Association for State & Local History · Society of American Historians

CONTENTS   *February 1961 · Volume XII, Number 2*

COVER: What prosperous, status-seeking merchant, in the mid-nineteenth century, did not aspire to those badges of achievement, a pair of fine horses, a Brewster buggy for summer, a handsome sleigh for winter, with the appropriate furs and sleigh bells, and, not least important, a lovely wife? Our cover—artist, subject, and locality unknown—was undoubtedly the work of an itinerant painter for just such a man, arrived at success and eager to record it. He was unusually fortunate to have found an artist of such genuine ability, whose spirited and painstaking rendition of husband, wife, sleigh, and furs is now owned by the Wadsworth Atheneum in Hartford, Connecticut, where it forms a part of the Ella Gallup Sumner and Mary Catlin Sumner Collection. *Back Cover:* The custom of exchanging comic caricatures, on the occasion of St. Valentine's Day, seems to have been in vogue as early as the 1820's. Certainly it was high in popular favor by the time of the Civil War, the date of this colorful trio of colonel, captain, and swashbuckling soldier from the Kean Archives, Philadelphia.

WHEN THE RED STORM BROKE

To a Russia in revolution, America sent rival groups of amateur diplomats. The calamitous results of their indecision still afflict us

By WILLIAM HARLAN HALE

In the early days of November, 1917, a wiry, abbreviated man bearing on his face the expression of a determined ferret and in his pocket an important commission from President Woodrow Wilson, stopped off in London at the Savoy Hotel, then noisy with officers on leave from the western front and a banjo band straight from Dixie. He soon heard disconcerting news. "Vague word of a strange new Russian disturbance called Bolshevik" (so he was to recall in his memoirs) had begun to permeate London. "Petrograd became silent. Accounts from points outside Russia were murky and contradictory. The American Embassy was no better informed than others."

Among the least informed was the traveler himself, which was somewhat ironic, since he was momentarily on his way direct to Petrograd as a supposed expert on information, propaganda, and counterintelligence. The October Revolution was fought and won before Edgar Sisson, the special Petrograd representative of President Wilson's wartime Committee on Public Information, ever got wind of it.

A Soviet artist glorified the violence of the Bolshevik mob that stormed the Petrograd Winter Palace, where the ineffectual parliamentary government of Alexander Kerensky sat. Kerensky himself managed to flee in a caravan led by a car and chauffeur commandeered from the American Embassy.

Sisson, a minor and now forgotten actor who briefly blundered onto center stage in an erupting world, is interesting historically only as a symbol. He stands, so to speak, for the shortcomings of American diplomacy at one catastrophic moment. And further, he represents what could be called the Great Russo-American Reversal of 1917–18, which brought to an end our century-old friendly relations with a czarist empire remote from our interests but hitherto benevolent to our own republican growth. When social upheaval toppled the Autocrat of all the Russias in early 1917, the United States believed that the old relations would continue as before, but the events of late 1917 doomed these simple hopes. When Red Russia threatened to leave the war against the Kaiser's Germany just after we had gotten into it, and next threatened to substitute for that war of nations a war of classes—to be fomented even inside America as well—the sudden reversal reached its climax. A few shattering months led to a total breakdown of communications between Russia and America, to the point where the two hitherto cordial peoples and governments on opposite sides of the globe grew so riddled with mutual fears and suspicion as to become all but incomprehensible to one another. From this situation, as everyone knows, we have never really recovered; the few intervals of *rapprochement* over the years have all turned out to be false dawns, and we still live under the sign of that darkness which descended between the two contrasting world powers in the bitter winter of 1917–18.

Did it have to happen—or happen as it did? Historians keep sifting the evidence, each through his own sieve. All agree that revolutionary Russia provided the challenge; what remains at issue is the shrewdness, the imagination, and the wisdom of America's response. In its upheaval, the far-off empire that we had so long looked upon as the legendary haven of the ikon and the muzhik suddenly swung into America's ken with a spectacle of total disorder and social threat. The shock was great, and a surprised and inexperienced America responded to it with its own spectacle of

"At no time was there any likelihood of our recognizing the Bolshevik Soviet Government. . . . I never saw Trotsky. I saw Lenin on one occasion."
David R. Francis
American Ambassador

confusion and disorder, presented first of all right on the ground of Petrograd.

For it was there, even before the guns went off and snows and machine-gun nests clogged the wintry streets, that our troubles with the new Russia began. The United States, a newcomer to great-power politics, had been content to choose, as the great majority of its emissaries, rank amateurs—in the form of deserving campaign contributors, political pensioners, and an occasional hungry intellectual seeking a paid-for existence overseas. When Russia erupted in such a violent and confusing way, we did not greatly change our manner of selecting diplomats; we simply sent more of them. The result was that America descended upon Petrograd with such a cloud of assorted troubleshooters, visiting firemen, adventurers, and idealists as had never before been seen in the relations between civilized states—each of them independent of the next, and all of them amateur. Therewith began a new stage of American diplomacy under threat of crisis—that of mass deployment abroad designed to conceal by sheer numbers underlying cross-purposes and indecision at home.

President Franklin D. Roosevelt, in the succeeding generation, was to prove himself a past master of this tactic of sending out multiple and often mutually contradictory emissaries, and then letting the pieces fall where they might; but President Wilson, fresh in the exercise of American world power, was the pioneer.

Perhaps never before had one nation dispatched to another in times of the latter's travail such a mixed company of the unskilled and innocent, with so little knowledge and preparation for what lay ahead. Nor had so many American diplomats ever gone forth with such lack of concerted purpose. Ridden with rivalries and cross-purposes that added to the general misunderstandings now arising between the United States and Russia, these multiple envoys were no match for the monolithic Lenin and Trotsky, who knew precisely what they wanted; and the end result of a winter's tortuous efforts in Petrograd was the breakdown of relations that had existed between the two countries for over a century.

The "strange new disturbance" of which Sisson wrote, referring to the Bolsheviks, had been making itself felt for quite some time before his arrival there, and with increasing virulence for fully seven months—in fact, ever since the Czar's war-battered regime had collapsed in March, 1917, and given way to a Provisional government of republican reformists. But it had not as yet penetrated the consciousness of faraway Washington. Indeed, practically all America, then just entering upon its crusade against the Kaiser's autocratic Germany, had hailed the Czar's abdication as the removal of an autocratic incubus on our own side, and—upon receiving confident advice from our Embassy in Russia—had fully believed through the summer and into the fall of 1917 that such enlightened new leaders as Prince Lvov and Alexander Kerensky would democratize Russian institutions, rebuild fighting morale, and make of their nation a worthy partner of ours in a common cause. This was the dream; and

"Found Ambassador without policy except anger at Bolsheviks, unamenable to arguments or entreaties of his official advisers. . . . I recommend . . . establishment of working, informal contact with de facto power by official representatives."
Edgar Sisson
Special Envoy

here was one of its carriers, Sisson, chosen for his mission because of his stature as one of America's most astute journalists (editor of the *Cosmopolitan Magazine* and, before that, managing editor of *Collier's*), passing through London with little inkling of what had been occurring under the surface farther east and none at all as to where this was now about to lead.

On November 25, after making his way across a U-boat-infested North Sea and a wintry Scandinavia, he reached the Russian capital's Finland Station.

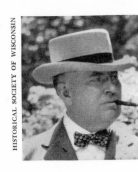

"Distribute the damned land and settle the compensation afterward."
William B. Thompson
Red Cross Mission Head

There he found, as he bounced in his sleigh over the icy hummocks of the Liteiny Prospekt and turned down the Furshtatskaya to the American Embassy, a city of dim-lit streets, tight-shuttered windows, and long-coated, muffled figures with rifles warming themselves before wood fires at the intersections. These were no policemen of a friendly, Provisional Kerensky; these were the Red Guards of the Petrograd Soviet of V. I. Lenin, who had arrived at the Finland Station too (but half a year earlier than Sisson) and who, while the bemused American editor was traveling, had seized the capital and then all Russia as well. Almost overnight Kerensky had been toppled by the Bolshevik Revolution of October, 1917 (November, by the Western calendar). Russia's ill-used armies were melting away, as the slogan "Peace, Bread, and Land" resounded through their ranks; banks, businesses, church properties, great estates were being seized. Moreover, the very day after Sisson arrived in Petrograd, bearing vague and now antiquated general instructions which he summed up as meaning "To be helpful to Russia in any practical way that might develop" and "To place before Russians the American viewpoint on the waging . . . of the war," Lenin's Commissar for Foreign Affairs, Leon Trotsky, formally appealed to the German high command for an armistice.

When Sisson took up quarters in the Embassy building—a low, sprawling monstrosity in a once-fashionable street, whose imitation-classical friezes, swollen balustrades, misbegotten balconies, and squashed-down mansard roof embodied the worst taste of the recent Romanov past—he found it stuffed to the rafters with a small army of assorted Americans as confused and at

loose ends as he, and, moreover, at loggerheads with one another.

There were four other key and contrasting men at the core of the American official colony in Petrograd: the Ambassador, David R. Francis, an elderly St. Louis grain dealer and Democratic politician; William Boyce Thompson, a multimillionaire copper magnate, promoter, and flamboyant high-liver, who headed the American Red Cross Commission to Russia; Thompson's deputy, Raymond Robins, a fiery Chicago social reformer and Progressive party orator with Indian blood in his veins, who had made a fortune in the Alaska gold rush; and Brigadier General William V. Judson, military attaché—the only one of them who had had any previous experience of Russia or even of foreign service, having witnessed the Russo-Japanese War as a military observer. Of these, Ambassador Fran-

"When every evil rumor becomes foundation for distrust, co-operation is impossible."
Raymond Robins
Thompson's Deputy

cis should have been, by virtue of his position, the dominant and controlling personality. That he was not —that he became in fact the very opposite—was due partly to his own shortcomings and partly to the Washington approach to appointments abroad that was both frivolous and chaotic.

In times past America had sent to Russia both some very good envoys and some very bad ones, the range extending all the way from the masterly John Quincy Adams and the scholarly Andrew D. White to the alcoholic John Randolph, the notoriously corrupt Simon Cameron, and that boisterous showman from border Kentucky, Cassius M. Clay, who in President Lincoln's day liked to sport his pearl-handled bowie knife at the Czar's court. In this ill-assorted gallery, David R. Francis was not as outrageous as some who had preceded him; he was simply quaint and totally miscast for his job. A mayor of St. Louis back in the rough-and-tumble 1880's, and then governor of Missouri, he looked like a period piece out of those days, with his white mane, high stand-up collar, and thick gold watch chain; his tastes ran to long evenings of poker, and during the ten days that shook the world, he sometimes seemed to be concerned chiefly with maintaining his supply of bourbon and cigars. In the delicious portrait George F. Kennan paints of him in *Russia Leaves the War*,

"The time of protests and threats addressed to the Soviet Government has passed, if indeed there ever was such a time. . . ."
General W. V. Judson
Military Mission Chief

the author suspects that the legend of Francis' "portable cuspidor, with its clanking, foot-operated lid may have been apocryphal," but recounts the Ambassador's custom of accompanying his diplomatic dinners with records played on a squeaky gramophone behind a screen, with his Negro butler and confidant "interrupting the service at table from time to time to crank it," all to the astonishment of the guests.

Elderly as he was, the amiable grain dealer sent out by the Calvinist Woodrow Wilson was not too old to indulge his tastes in another direction—which resulted in one of the more grotesque indiscretions in the chronicles of American diplomacy. While the eyes of the world were focused apprehensively on the progress of Lenin's uprising, cables hurried between Washington and Petrograd on the subject of the American ambassador's relationship with a certain Mme. Matilda de Cram. This handsome lady had sought out Francis' acquaintance aboard ship while he was on his way without his family to his post, and subsequently became a constant visitor of his at the Embassy. It was understood that she was giving him French lessons. All might have been well, in the worldly environment of continental diplomacy, save that Mme. de Cram, the wife of a Russian officer, was strongly suspected by Russian authorities of being a German agent. She was also on the secret suspect list of the Inter-Allied Passport Agency. General Judson, who was particularly concerned about her proximity to coded messages and code books when in the Ambassador's private presence, finally confronted Francis with the stories going round about her—only to be told to mind his own business. Then someone at the Embassy directly informed the State Department, which took the extraordinary step of requesting Francis to discontinue his relationship with Mme. de Cram. To this Francis replied crustily that the lady in question hadn't visited him for quite some time. A second exchange took place; then the department, realizing that to remove Francis, a deserving Democrat, might produce a scandal, sent him a mollifying cable welcoming his information that Mme. de Cram's visits had ceased. End of episode —and whether she was in fact what she was suspected of being has never been substantiated.

While these intramural exchanges were going on, Lenin and Trotsky had entered upon somewhat more significant ones with the German high command at Brest-Litovsk. It was midwinter; they sought a separate peace and were about to dissolve the multiparty Constituent Assembly at Petrograd in order to establish a complete Bolshevik dictatorship over Russia. The Ambassador, however, who had rarely ventured out of his Embassy during the explosive days of No-

vember, made no personal contact with either of the new Russian chiefs. In this he was acting on instructions from Washington on December 6 to refrain from such contact—instructions which, however, were in effect just Francis talking to Francis, since they had been drafted in response to his own cabled advice, the burden of which over many months had been that he saw no point in talking with the Bolsheviks. They were a minority agitational group, he explained, and evidently not here to stay.

As time off from poker and Mme. de Cram allowed, Francis had kept informing the President and Secre-

The road to ruin of the moderate Kerensky (right) was paved with idealistic intentions and American hopes. Here, during his brief moment of glory in 1917, he reviews his troops.

tary of State Robert Lansing of his satisfaction with the way matters in Russia were proceeding under Kerensky. Thus on May 31, 1917: "Kerensky is still continuing his inspection of the front, and is met everywhere with the greatest enthusiasm." "Enthusiasm," however, had been hardly the right word with which to describe the state of mind of Russia's sullen conscripts, then on the verge of throwing down their guns. Meanwhile the Ambassador's private, conservative predilections had run much deeper; soon after Kerensky took power in March of 1917, Francis had written one of his chief deputies, Consul General Maddin Summers at Moscow (a Foreign Service professional who held high prestige in Francis' eyes because of his marriage into a highly connected czarist family), "I am much pleased to hear that the President of the [new] Ministry, [Prince] Lvov, is a first cousin of your mother-in-law and that other members of the Ministry are connected with your family. . . . I have been of the opinion that it would be unwise to attempt to establish a republican form of government in Russia just now, but if such men as these are put at the helm, it is possible they may be able to steer through the breakers . . ."

It seems never to have occurred to President Wilson that an envoy of such predilections might become a drawback in exploding Russia, and that he should be replaced. Instead, vaguely uneasy, Wilson had begun in the spring of 1917 to send out numbers of other missions, commissions, and individuals to strengthen Francis' and America's hand there—although none of these was responsible to the chief missionary on the ground.

The decision of Kerensky's Bolshevik successors, Lenin (left) and Trotsky, to make a separate peace with the German government earned the immediate hostility of the Allies.

Would Kerensky's Russia keep fighting the Germans? Wilson, whose lack of knowledge of that far country was as conspicuous as his command of political processes at home, had dispatched in May a nine-man fact-finding and good-will committee headed by the venerable Republican ex-Secretary of State, Elihu Root. Mr. Root's mandate was simply to display to troubled Russia America's "sympathy and interest," and he was hardly an ideal choice: he had confessed before setting out that he expected to be "awfully bored" there, and after a month-long round of receptions and banquets with Provisional ministers, during which he and his fellow committeemen disdained contact with the emerging Left, he returned home to deliver a bland report saying that Russia was out of danger and could be relied on. Almost simultaneously, another American delegation descended upon Russia—also without invitation: a task force of eminent American railroad men, arriving to lend advice on how to strengthen the deposed Czar's floundering transportation system. The prospect of American dollar aid was

invigorating to Kerensky's officials, but the presence of so many Americans at once was rather crushing to their working hours and protocol. What next?

Next came the Red Cross Commission—and a group of men with more unusual designs under the cross of Geneva had never set foot from one nation into another. William Boyce Thompson, the squat, thickset victor of many a stock-market raid and Montana mining scheme, was one of many Americans anxious in that spring of 1917 to get into the war. As his biographer, Hermann Hagedorn, recalls:

His friends were already deep in [it] as field-marshals and ambassadors. Baruch, on the Council for National Defense, was wielding dictatorial power in the economic field. . . . Henry P. Davison [a partner of the House of Morgan], as head of the American Red Cross, was dramatizing the code of the Samaritan on an almost mythical scale. Thompson no longer found promotions and stock operations stimulating enough for his imagination. . . . The overthrow of the Czar startled and thrilled him. Russia would be the decisive factor in the war, he said. If Russia could be held firm, Germany would be defeated. If the Russian front broke—. . .

So Thompson approached his friend Davison, then projecting a Red Cross relief mission to Russia, to propose that he himself go along on it—not, indeed, simply to help supervise the distribution of foodstuffs and blankets, but to enlarge its scope immensely, its goal to be nothing less than to shore up the Provisional regime. Thompson, whose means were as spacious as his dreams, offered to pay all costs of the mission himself! The proposal was dazzling, and no one seems quite to have sensed the implications of letting a private relief body mix in with high politics abroad. The President, casting about for at least some way of influencing the course of affairs in Russia, gave the scheme his blessing, and before midsummer a party of some twenty experts, all decked out for the occasion in military uniforms and sporting assimilated military titles, was on its way across the Pacific to Vladivostok.

Kerensky's people had let it be known that they did not see the need of an American Red Cross mission: their own hospitals and food supplies were adequate, thank you. Ambassador Francis also opposed it, fearing (quite rightly, as it turned out) that it would trespass on his own domain. Yet the caravan came on. Before its departure, though, Davison startled Thompson—now "Colonel" Thompson—by including on the roster a Chicago Progressive friend of Theodore Roosevelt. Having refused to let the ex-President lead an infantry division in France, the Administration was trying to appease him.

"What! Raymond Robins, that uplifter, that Roosevelt shouter!" exploded Thompson on learning of the

CONTINUED ON PAGE 100

American Athens

to cosmopolitan capital of the Republic—this was Philadelphia's first century

Until he journeyed to Philadelphia in 1774 to attend the meetings of the First Continental Congress, John Adams had never been out of his native New England. He had even been thinking of quietly retiring to his Braintree farm when the explosive atmosphere in and about Boston (watchful redcoats camped on the Common that summer) thrust him from his own beleaguered part of the world into the main stream of large affairs —and into the most cosmopolitan, progressive, and affluent society in colonial America.

Adams' first opinions of the wider world that he observed along the banks of the Delaware were not altogether charitable. It was a world of differences, and, taking Boston as his criterion, he felt that it left much to be desired. To the delegate from Massachusetts the easy tolerance of Philadelphians was heterodoxy. Their general well-being was tainted by prodigality. Tested with the strong dye of Yankee Congregationalism, the city's confusion of religious sects, the medley of disparate cultures, and the babble of strange accents indicated grave impurities in the social body. For all its "trade and wealth and regularity," Adams concluded after a brief survey, Philadelphia was *not* Boston. "The morals of our people are much better," he confided to his diary; "their manners are more polite and agreeable; they are purer English; our language is better, our taste is better, our persons are handsomer; our spirit is greater, our laws are wiser, our religion is superior, our education is better."

Local pride can be a useful social force, but Adams carried it to an extreme that "tinctured his judgment and clinched his prepossessions." No one, to be sure, would have mistaken the flourishing city of Philadelphia, so neatly and spaciously arranged on its tree-lined checkerboard, for the closed port of Boston, with its crooked, narrow streets echoing to the tramp of

No record survives of Penn's historic 1683 treaty with the Indians, a covenant that was neither signed nor sworn to, and never broken. Thomas Birch's painting, left, is an imaginative reconstruction of Penn's arrival in this country.

soldiers' boots, its populace exasperated almost to the point of open revolt. As to morals, manners, and the other items on Adams' uncompromising list of particulars, it was evidently easier to detect the differences than to understand their meaning. As Montaigne wrote of the disparaging reports he had heard of the New World, it is all too simple to call any divergence from custom a barbarism and let it go at that. Philadelphia was not like Boston; in many significant ways it was not like any other place on earth.

It was, in fact, a prodigy. Within less than a century after its beginnings, William Penn's "green countrie towne" had become the most populous and consequential city in the British colonies and stood among the first half-dozen in the empire. No city in history had grown to maturity so rapidly and so handsomely. While Philadelphia was a-borning, St. Petersburg was created by imperial fiat almost overnight on the swamp of the Neva (at an enormous cost in human suffering), so that Peter the Great might have a showplace with a window from which to look out over western Europe. But St. Petersburg was a throwback to the Paris of the Grand Monarch; Philadelphia was a portent of the future.

At Philadelphia those "schismatical factious" Quakers, a sect whose members had earlier been whipped and dragged through the streets of Boston and hanged on the Common, had opened the doors of Pennsylvania to the entire world. Here, Penn promised, would be a "free colony for all mankind." And although all history and experience denied it, he cherished the notion that men of good will could govern themselves. By royal proclamation he was absolute proprietor, but he wrote his subjects: "You shall be governed by laws of your own makeing, and live a free, and if you will, a sober and industreous People. I shall not usurp the right of any, or oppress his person. God has furnisht me with a better resolution, and has given me his grace to keep it. . . . I am your true Friend."

Early reports about the Society of Friends had made converts as far away as Russia. Penn himself had visited the Rhineland, and his letters and brochures, translated and widely circulated, sent vast numbers

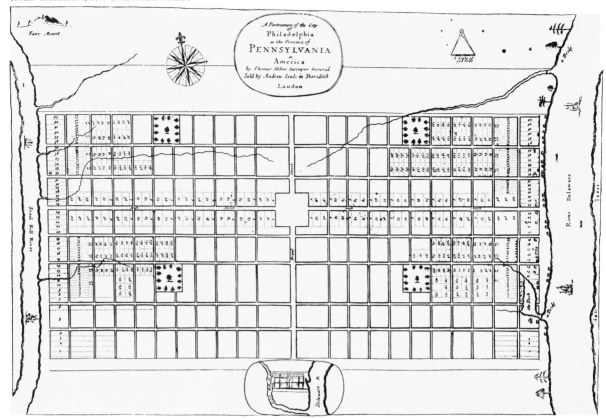

Philadelphia's town plan, an urban gridiron drawn between two rivers, was one of America's earliest. Forty years after Thomas Holme's original survey (above), Peter Cooper's painting of the city's skyline (below) showed it to have become a bustling metropolis. Affluent, high-living Quaker merchants, "full of all Country business and Sea affairs," built homes in a stately procession on Front Street, near the wharves and stores along the Delaware.

of discontented German peasants swarming across the Atlantic. The Scotch-Irish Presbyterians from Ulster needed little encouragement to flock to this promised land where neither the Irish "papists" nor the Established Anglicans could hope to influence their lives and their convictions. In 1729 James Logan, Secretary of the Province, began to fear these "Protestants of the Protestants" might take control of the colony and the Quakers become victims of their own liberal policies. At mid-century Benjamin Franklin feared it might rather be the Germans. These latter continued to arrive in a steady stream; in 1738 alone some nine thousand newcomers from the upper Rhine disembarked at Philadelphia, and most of them spread out over the black soil of the hinterland.

Dutchmen, Swedes, and Finns had already been in Penn's land and had helped the first English colonists to settle there. From the exposed frontiers of other colonies harassed settlers were drawn to "this peaceable kingdom." At one point neighboring Maryland was obliged to post a patrol along its border to prevent deserters from the British fleet in Baltimore from slipping away into Pennsylvania. Ben Franklin, of course, escaped to Philadelphia from the heart of Boston, and added a new, strong, and highly individual strain to the conglomeration.

"We are a people, thrown together from various quarters of the world," reported William Smith, the Scottish Provost of the College of Philadelphia and the "Great Cham" of the city's literary life, "differing in all things—language, manners, and sentiments. We are blessed with privileges, which to the wise will prove a sanctuary, but to the foolish a rock of offense." Here it was most evident that, as Tom Paine pointed out, Europe, not England, was the parent country of America.

There was enough quarreling and contention among the various factions to keep the community in a healthy ferment. On the other hand, virtually everyone, regardless of his individual persuasions, had a solid stake in this thriving society, and there was enough widely scattered good sense to realize it and to keep the melting pot from boiling over. Penn had all but lifted the curse of the Tower of Babel. The revolutionary implications of that liberation were not lost on the philosophers of the eighteenth century. Philadelphia was the Enlightenment in a microcosm. At last, Voltaire exulted, there was reasonable proof for an age of reason that men of mixed origins and different beliefs could live together on terms of equality, and prosper. Penn's experiment had, in effect, become a prospectus of the America to be.

In June, 1776, this was emphatically demonstrated before the delegates to the Second Continental Congress, then sitting in Philadelphia, when the "radical" elements of the colony—the frontiersmen and city workmen, the "little" people of diverse foreign strains and others of "native" English stock who had hitherto

TEXT CONTINUED ON PAGE 103
A PORTFOLIO OF ILLUSTRATIONS APPEARS ON THE FOLLOWING PAGES

A View of the House of Employment, Alms-house

A. The Managers Apartment
B.B. The House of Employment
C.C. The Alms House.
D. The Pensylvania Hospital

Notable

The public buildings of Philadelphia were monuments to the humanitarianism and the enlightened spirit of the Quakers. At the left in the engraved view above is the House of Employment and Almshouse—the so-called Bettering House—built and largely supported by private contributions. It was considered "one of the principal Ornaments" of Philadelphia when it was completed in the fall of 1767. The Pennsylvania Hospital, shown at the right, was opened to patients in 1756 and quickly attracted medical students from all parts of the continent. With its accommodations for lunatics, its sanitary arrange-

Pensylvania Hospital, & part of the City of Philadelphia

The State House

Christ's Church

g.The new Building or Presbⁿ Church

h. The German School House.

i. The New Dutch Church Steple.

k. The Court House.

Public Works

ments, and its enlightened administration, it was probably the most advanced institution of its kind then known. William Russell Birch's view of Independence Hall (left) shows America's most hallowed historic structure before the present steeple was added. When first used in 1735, although unfinished, it was the largest and handsomest public building in the colonies. Philadelphia was the first major city to build an adequate public water system. At right is Birch's painting of the marble station at Centre Square, designed by Benjamin Henry Latrobe, to house the pumps that distributed the Schuylkill's water.

15

*The
Pulse
of City
Life*

At the turn of the century, in 1799 and 1800, Birch and his son Thomas issued a series of engraved views of Philadelphia that provide a remarkable record of the most attractive and the most enterprising of eighteenth-century American cities. At the time the Birches pictured it, the junction of Second and High streets (left) marked the heart of Philadelphia. Distances from the city to other places were measured from this intersection. In another view (above) they recorded the procession commemorating the death of Washington as it passed by the country market place on High Street. The Arch Street Ferry is shown below. In 1797 more than 1,400 vessels berthed at bustling Philadelphia.

The Good Citizen

Benjamin Franklin was the most cosmopolitan spirit of his age. The self-made republican, the tallow-chandler's son, the many-sided tradesman, and the universal genius moved with grace and honor among the powdered heads of Europe, quipping with royalty and corresponding at once easily and profoundly with the greatest intellects of the day.

Born in Boston, whither his parents had moved from Nantucket (he liked to explain that his keel had been laid in Nantucket but that he had been launched in Boston), he spent a great many of his mature years in England and France. Yet this tireless man of the world was completely at home in his adopted city of Philadelphia and was intimately involved in its problems and projects. He gave the impetus to practically every undertaking that advanced the welfare and the importance of the city in his time. With his printing press, his remarkably lucid literary style, and his uncommonly good sense, he was an unmatched propagandist for worthy causes. When the good citizens of Philadelphia proved reluctant to subscribe to the radical proposal to found a modern public hospital, Dr. Thomas Bond appealed to Franklin. "There is no such thing," Bond wrote, "as carrying through a public-spirited project without you are concerned with it; for I am often asked by those to whom I propose subscribing, 'Have you consulted Franklin on this business? And what does he think of it?'" Here, as in so many other concerns, Franklin's persuasive influence, usually leavened by the best of humor, was the vital ingredient of success.

And he was concerned with almost everything. On a single day in 1772 he wrote thirteen letters to as many different persons on subjects that ranged from the employment problems of a glass factory and the problems of silk culture to the selection of books for the Library Company and the principle of oath-taking. He sometimes covered almost as much ground in one letter. The Library Company of Philadelphia was itself an outgrowth of his Junto, a club of thoughtful young tradesmen whom Franklin brought together in 1727, as was the Union Fire Company, founded in 1736, the first in town and the beginning of a flourishing city-wide system of protection.

Like a pebble thrown in a pond, Franklin caused a series of ever-widening circles that finally ringed the city with public-spirited endeavor. Thus he was at the center of the movements that reformed the city watch, improved the paving, cleaning, and lighting of streets, gave birth to the Academy that became the University of Pennsylvania, and organized the military defenses of the Quaker province.

Out of Franklin's Junto, too, emerged the American Philosophical Society, a symbol of the smouldering intellectual curiosity which he fanned into a bright flame by his own incessant investigation of the world he lived in, the seen and the unseen. His invention of the lightning rod, deemed by some contemporaries a sacrilegious interference with God's plan for mankind, was only one of the experiments by which he attracted to Philadelphia the attention of the scientific world. On another level, the maxims of Poor Richard that emanated from Franklin's press won world-wide currency.

Art as well stood in Franklin's debt. Letters from Dr. Franklin had helped young Benjamin West get established in London, nor did his friendship flag as West became court painter to George III and the monarch's intimate friend. Despite war and political struggles, three generations of American artists studied in London under the kindly, hospitable West. He became the most widely known American painter of his day, perhaps of history, and in 1805 he paid his compliments to the memory of his friend with the allegorical painting at right, showing the Philadelphia genius, attended by cherubim, snatching lightning from the heavens.

Benjamin Rush, by Thomas Sully

Men of Mind
and
Substance

Except for its distance from the Old World's courts and capitals, there was little that was provincial about Philadelphia in the second half of the eighteenth century. Although Franklin's enormous reputation tended to overshadow the attainments of his fellow citizens, the city abounded in men of brilliant minds, some of them as highly regarded in Europe as they were in America. Benjamin Rush was the most prominent American physician of his day and the foremost teacher of medicine. Following his graduation from the University of Edinburgh and further training in London, he occupied the first chair in chemistry in the colonies, at the College of Philadelphia. A man of many parts, master of a clear literary style, and unafraid of the controversies he sparked by his original opinions, he promoted interest in such varied matters as psychiatry, abolition, prison reform, temperance, and female education. It was he who urged Thomas Paine to write *Common Sense* and suggested the title. And he proudly signed the Declaration of Independence.

One of his teachers, Dr. John Morgan, was another man of the world of science, a member of many distinguished foreign societies and a founder of the medical school in Philadelphia. With his wealthy companion Samuel Powel, Morgan made the grand tour of Europe in the grandest manner and had studied in Paris and Italy as well as in London and Edinburgh. He first defined the separate concerns of the physician, the surgeon, and the apothecary, a degree of specialization that was then considered revolutionary and that furthered his fame.

David Rittenhouse, one of Charles Willson Peale's many subjects, was a self-taught instrument maker, astronomer, and mathematician whose genius shone as brightly as that of any of his formally educated contemporaries. His two celebrated orreries, ingenious prototypes of our modern planetariums, won him an enormous reputation. He made the first telescope in America, helped both Washington and Jefferson in their scientific problems, and acted as a one-man bureau of standards. Upon Franklin's death, he became the American Philosophical Society's president.

Joseph Priestley, "an eighteenth-century Bertrand Russell," found refuge in Pennsylvania after a Birmingham mob, incensed by his liberal notions, burned his home and books. He first published the story of Franklin and his kite. He made fundamental contributions to education, theology, and chemistry, among them the "invention" of oxygen. To escape the banquets of Philadelphia, he retired to a quiet, productive life in Northumberland on the Susquehanna.

Dr. John Morgan, by T. S. Duché

David Rittenhouse, by Charles Willson Peale

By Order of His Excellency

Sir William Howe, K. B.

General and Commander in Chief, &c. &c. &c.

PROCLAMATION.

I DO hereby give Notice to the Inhabitants of the City of Philadelphia and its Environs, it is the Order of His Excellency, that " No Person whatever, living " within the said City and its Environs, shall appear in " the Streets between the Beating of the Tattoo, at Half " an Hour after Eight o'Clock in the Evening, and the " Revellie in the Morning, without Lanthorns: And all " who shall be found abroad, within the Time aforesaid, " will be liable to be examined by the Patroles, and con- " fined, unless they shall give a satisfactory Account of " themselves." And I do hereby enjoin and require the Inhabitants, and all others residing in the said City and its Environs, to pay strict Obedience to the said Order, and govern themselves accordingly.

Given under my Hand at Philadelphia, this 9th Day of January, in the Eighteenth Year of His Majesty's Reign.   JOS. GALLOWAY,
Superintendent-General.

The scene in Independence Hall as the Continental Congress voted for independence (above) was painted by Robert Edge Pine and Edward Savage some years after that historic occasion. Fourteen months after the Declaration was issued, General Howe moved into Philadelphia. The painting by Xavier Della Gatta (opposite page) pictures the action about Benjamin Chew's house on the Germantown Road as Washington gallantly but unsuccessfully tried to loosen the redcoats' hold on the city.

There were enough Tories and lonely girls in Philadelphia to make it a pleasant winter for the British troops, while Washington retired to the miseries of Valley Forge. When Howe was called home to England to report, Major André and twenty other officers subscribed £3,312 to stage a farewell party, the Mischianza (opposite page, bottom), of such extravagant splendor as America had never seen and, as one of the weary belles ruefully concluded, would probably never see again.

In Council of Safety.

Philadelphia, December 2, 1776.

RESOLVED,

THAT it is the Opinion of this Board, that all the Shops in this City be shut up, that the Schools be broke up, and the Inhabitants engaged solely in providing for the Defence of this City, at this Time of extreme Danger.

By Order of Council,

DAVID RITTENHOUSE, Vice-President.

[Philadelphia, Printed by Henry Miller, in Race-street.]

Annals of Philadelphia, VOL. II, BY J. F. WATSON (1884 ED.)

The modishness and the wit of the ladies of Philadelphia were both celebrated and criticized. Young John Quincy Adams, shortly after his return from Russia, thought that attractive women were almost commonplace in the Quaker city. Thomas Jefferson admired Mrs. Bingham's keen mind and good sense as much as he appreciated her beauty. John Adams, on the other hand, wrote growlingly from Philadelphia that "the *femmes savantes* are contemptible characters"; and his wife complained that the décolleté ladies, "not content with the *show which* nature bestows, . . . borrow from art, and litterally look like Nursing Mothers."

Gilbert Stuart's unfinished portrait of Mrs. William Bingham (née Anne Willing), above, is one of his several attempts to record the almost legendary beauty of Philadelphia's most renowned hostess. After five years in which, solidly supported by her indulgent husband's large fortune, she displayed a "passion and thirst after all the luxuries of Europe," this young lady ruled the city's society for the decade that Philadelphia remained the national capital. "Less money and more years may make her wiser," wrote Abigail Adams, "but she is so handsome she must be pardoned." Both at her city home and at Lansdowne (right), her elaborate country seat, her lavish entertainments introduced a courtly atmosphere disturbing to earnest republicans. The elopement of her 15-year-old daughter with a dissipated French count was a shock from which she barely recovered before her death at 37.

24

Ladies Houses

In 1797 the Duc de Liancourt wrote: "The profusion and luxury of Philadelphia on great days, at the tables of the wealthy, in their equipages, and the dresses of their wives and daughters, are extreme. I have seen balls on the President's birthday where the splendor . . . did not suffer in comparison with Europe; and it must be acknowledged that the beauty of the American ladies has the advantage in the comparison. The young women of Philadelphia are accomplished in different degrees, but beauty is general with them. They want the ease and fashion of French women, but the brilliancy of their complexion is infinitely superior."

OLD PRINT SHOP

Peggy Shippen, above, had neither the extravagant beauty nor the brilliant style of Anne Willing Bingham. She had enough attractions, however, to catch the eye and win the heart of General Benedict Arnold when Washington placed that wounded hero in command of Philadelphia in 1778, following the British evacuation of the city. The two were married in the spring of the next year and almost at once hatched plans to betray their country. Arnold was a disgruntled warrior, Peggy a Loyalist at heart. When André's capture disclosed the treason, Peggy was banished from Pennsylvania. Daniel Gardner painted this portrait of her with one of her children during her exile in London. In 1789 she returned briefly to her father's handsome brick house on South Second Street (left), the home of her childhood, but hostile public opinion drove her back to England, where she died in 1804.

Ardor
for the
Arts

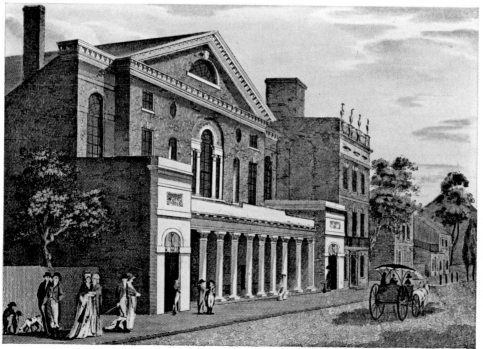

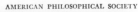

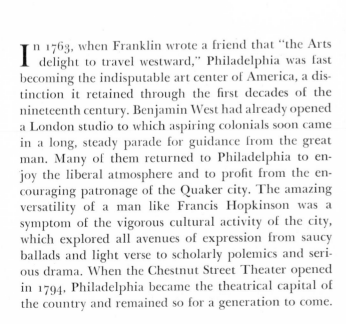

The American School (*left*), *painted by Matthew Pratt in 1755, most famous of American conversation pieces, shows West in his London studio correcting Pratt's drawing while other young colonial artists look on. Charles Willson Peale pictured himself (above, right) as he appeared about 1777– 78 in his militiaman's uniform and captain's hat. Almost twenty years later, with the help of his son Rembrandt, he painted a candid likeness of Gilbert Stuart (above, left) which that witty genius did not appreciate. Robert Edge Pine's portrait below is a thoughtful study of Francis Hopkinson, Philadelphia's first dilettante—a composer, balladeer, essayist, poet, satirist, and painter. He was also an admiralty judge and a signer of the Declaration. William Birch pictured the Chestnut Street Theater (opposite) as it appeared in its heyday. The celebrated structure, inspired by the playhouse in Bath, England, burned down in 1820.*

In 1763, when Franklin wrote a friend that "the Arts delight to travel westward," Philadelphia was fast becoming the indisputable art center of America, a distinction it retained through the first decades of the nineteenth century. Benjamin West had already opened a London studio to which aspiring colonials soon came in a long, steady parade for guidance from the great man. Many of them returned to Philadelphia to enjoy the liberal atmosphere and to profit from the encouraging patronage of the Quaker city. The amazing versatility of a man like Francis Hopkinson was a symptom of the vigorous cultural activity of the city, which explored all avenues of expression from saucy ballads and light verse to scholarly polemics and serious drama. When the Chestnut Street Theater opened in 1794, Philadelphia became the theatrical capital of the country and remained so for a generation to come.

"I am apt to believe," John Adams wrote his wife from Philadelphia, "that [the signing of the Declaration of Independence] will be celebrated by succeeding generations as the great anniversary festival. . . . It ought to be solemnized with pomp

and parade, with shows, games, sports, guns, bells, bonfires, and illuminations, from one end of this continent to the other, from this time forward, forevermore." J. L. Krimmel's painting shows Philadelphia's attempt to celebrate the Fourth in 1819.

The STORMING of the ALAMO

None of its defenders survived, so that legends obscure their fate. But the facts do no dishonor to these beleaguered men, sworn to fight on until the end "at the peril of our lives, liberties and fortunes"

By CHARLES RAMSDELL

Few battles in our history have had more reverberations than the siege and assault of the Alamo, and yet no battle of consequence has been so skimpily reported.

In this action fewer than 200 men, most of them Americans, were besieged by 3,000 Mexican troops in a fortress built on the ruins of a Spanish mission at San Antonio, in Texas, then a part of Mexico, from February 23 to March 6, 1836, when the walls were stormed and the defenders slaughtered to the last man.

None of the Mexican officers who witnessed the shambles cared to give a full account. The only plausible version of the final assault was written by the Mexican second-in-command, General Vicente Filisola, but he did not arrive until three days after the last shot had been fired.

The evidence about what happened at the Alamo is scattered. There is no bristling array of fact to inhibit the armchair theorist's romping fancy, and consequently writers—even scholars—have felt free to draw their picture of the action any way they pleased.

But recent writings give proof that a well-defined picture or stereotype has now emerged from the chaos of conflicting tales. According to this standard view, the Alamo was an indefensible ruin held, in defiance of superior orders, by a band of frontiersmen who were valiant but far from wise.

And yet, according to the evidence, the Alamo was "a strong place," and the defenders were in good part professional men; they disobeyed no orders, and their sacrifice was not without effect.

Let's look at the scattered evidence. Who were the men in the Alamo, and what were they doing there?

Few of the 150 "effective" men who went into the Alamo on February 23 at the approach of the Mexican army were Texans: most had been in the country less than a year. They had come singly or in small groups— a few had even walked—from the southwestern United States. But most of them were natives of the Atlantic seaboard. Some thirty-six were from the British Isles, including fourteen from Ireland. Two were Germans; one was a Dane.

But their officers, whose leadership they respected— or they would have chosen new ones—were well-known figures among the American colonists in Texas. Each had taken an active part, early or late, in the revolt. The men in the Alamo, therefore, were in sympathy with the Texas revolution, and had come to join it.

The revolution itself was not a conflict between "races" or peoples, nor between systems of government. Nor was it a conspiracy to steal Texas away from Mexico. To find the beginning—but not the meaning—of it, we must go back to the failure of Spain to take firm hold on Texas.

Even before the British fleet, Napoleon, and civil war had ripped the web of Spain's empire, there were not enough Spaniards in the Americas to hold down half a hemisphere. The wonder is that they were able to occupy Texas at all, considering the stark mountain ranges and grim deserts they had to cross coming northward from the opulent valleys of Mexico. Spain's hold on Texas was shaken in 1800, when Napoleon maneuvered a weak Spanish king out of Louisiana. When he sold his immense prize to the United States three years later, it was obvious that the Americans, as soon as they were settled in Louisiana itself, would begin to spill over into Texas, for it is attached by geography to the Mississippi Valley, with no natural barriers between.

Spain's policy for more than a century had been to keep Texas empty, a vast cushion of space to protect the rich mines of Mexico. An economical policy, it suited the king and worked fairly well for a time. Texas remained a vacuum.

But within the vacuum an unforeseen menace grew like a stormhead. The Comanche Indians, with 5,000 warriors, perhaps the most expert horsemen the world has known, roamed at will, lords of the prairie. In the whole reach of the province, counting the friendly Indians (who died off fast, inside and outside the missions, from the white man's diseases), there were scarcely 3,000 people who could be called subjects of Spain. Texas was at the mercy of the Comanche.

Forced to choose between the marauding Indians and the American frontiersmen who had begun trickling into Texas, the Spanish authorities chose the Americans. And in 1821 the commanding general of the frontier provinces, acting in the name of the king, granted to Moses Austin, a Connecticut Yankee turned Spanish subject, permission for an American colony.

In that same portentous year of 1821, Moses Austin died, leaving his Texas concession to his son, and Mexico declared its independence from Spain. Young Stephen F. Austin, in order to get clear title to his grant, had to petition each shaky new government as it arose, until the Mexican Republic, established in 1823 by men who admired the institutions of the United States, gave him full authority to settle American colonists in Texas.

He found some already there. Most of them scarcely hankered for annexation to the United States. Many had left home between suns, and the government they preferred was the one that governed least. That was Mexico, which levied no taxes, required no military service, and gave them land for the asking. They held the formidable Comanches in check. And so long as the government left them alone, the colonists seldom gave it a thought.

The government, however, began to grow more and more alarmed about the Americans in Texas, who rapidly outnumbered, and by far, the native population. The trickle from the east had become a steady stream, and in 1830 further immigration was prohibited. This and other repressive measures caused some violence but did not produce outright revolt. Even when Stephen Austin was arrested for urging the separation of Texas from Coahuila and confined in Mexico for a year and a half, there was no uproar. But when he reached home early in September of 1835, he found Texas in tumult.

In 1833, Antonio Lopez de Santa Anna, a bloody-minded royalist officer who had shifted with each political wind, had finally succeeded in seizing power in Mexico and subverting the high purpose of the republic's founders by establishing a military dictatorship. When he threatened to unleash an army of occupation on Texas, revolution flared. Mexican forces entered Texas from the coast in mid-September and occupied San Antonio—or Bexar, as it was called then—and Stephen Austin, usually a patient man, declared: "I will wear myself out inch by inch, rather than submit to the despotic rule of Santa Anna."

The revolution in Texas, as Austin made plain, was a stand against military dictatorship. The aim was not, in the beginning, independence from Mexico. The colonists, in a consultation at San Felipe de Austin on November 7, 1835, declared they had "taken up arms in defense of the federal constitution of Mexico of 1824." Only on March 2, 1836, while the Alamo was under bombardment, did a convention of colonists, held at Washington-on-Brazos, declare the independence of Texas.

The events of the preceding fall, when the colonists had begun their revolt, had gone badly for the forces of the Mexican government. On October 2, 1835, a detachment of Mexican troops from the garrison at San Antonio attempted to take a battered cannon from the colonists at Gonzales, the nearest American settlement, seventy miles to the east. The cannon belched defiance, and several soldiers were killed; the rest withdrew. Then colonists captured the fort at Goliad, near the coast, cutting the garrison at San Antonio off from the sea. From Gonzales a small motley army in buckskin, with Austin at its head, set out to capture San Antonio. On October 27 the advance guard led by James Bowie defeated an attacking force near Concepcion Mission, and the surviving Mexican troops took refuge behind the stone walls and palisades of the old Spanish town. The Americans' siege of San Antonio culminated in the house-to-house storming of the town from December 5 to 10 and in the surrender of the Mexican garrison, which was allowed to return across the Rio Grande with its arms.

While Austin's "army" was encamped outside the town, its numbers swelled to more than a thousand. And then, tired of inaction, most of the colonists went home. Austin himself, a sick man, resigned. Not more than 300 men took part in the storming.

Nearly half of those who were to become the defenders of the Alamo went through this ten-week campaign in the fall, then waited out the hard winter at San Antonio. They were abandoned, toward the last of December, by 200 victory-happy volunteers who headed south for the Gulf of Mexico, having been cajoled into an expedition aimed at seizing the port of Matamoros near the mouth of the Rio Grande—300 desolate miles away.

This ill-conceived, ill-fated Matamoros venture was intended to be the first step in a scheme to detach from Mexico all the rich mining states north of a line drawn straight west from Tampico, including the pauper state of Texas. The aim: to make, in collusion with Mexican politicos, a great new empire. The backers of this scheme were, of course, opposed to independence for Texas. Working through the provisional council, they succeeded in shunting aside early in January, 1836, the provisional governor, Henry Smith, and the commander in chief, General Sam Houston, both of whom were in favor of independence. Houston was stripped of power when the council made his subaltern, James W. Fannin, its agent, giving him all funds and all available manpower for a march on Matamoros.

Meanwhile, at San Antonio, 104 men were left destitute under Colonel J. C. Neill, who wrote to Governor Smith that the stampede for Matamoros had carried off most of the food, clothing, medicines, and the horses. Smith, in his log-cabin capital of San Felipe, 150 miles to the east, was already irked at the deal with Fannin and now vented his wrath on the council. This was what it was waiting for: an excuse to "depose" him. He in turn "dissolved" the council. Henceforth, until the convention met in March, the government of Texas was divided against itself. The result was disaster, at the Alamo and elsewhere.

Some at the Alamo, "not even sufficiently clad for summer," endured the winter "with but one blanket and one shirt." They had no money. "If there has ever been a dollar here," wrote Neill, "I have no knowledge of it." This was early in January, and the story is the same to the end: The men were not paid. In mid-January Neill reported he had only eighty "effective" men. The rest, apparently colonists, had gone home.

These eighty men had to garrison two distinct fortresses. In the town of San Antonio were the remnants of the Spanish fortress (on what is now Military Plaza), and a block to the east, with the old parish church in between, was the Civil Plaza (now Main). These dusty squares, surrounded by stone houses with flat roofs, had been fortified by the Mexican army in December.

Half a mile away, across the San Antonio River, which here makes a large bend to the east, was the Alamo. This was a compound of stone walls, with huts of adobe and "little houses of mud and stone" ranged along their inner sides, enclosing a bare and dusty area the size of a city block. There was a gateway on the south, and facing west on the enclosed area was a two-story stone building, the "long barracks." Behind this were two corrals walled with stone; and, south of these, a church—the "Alamo" of our day—facing west and making the southeast corner.

This drab enclosure comprised more than three acres. Built by Franciscan friars during the half-century after 1724 as a mission for Indians, it had been named San Antonio de Valero in honor of Saint Anthony of Padua and the reigning viceroy, the Marquis de Valero. It had long since been used as a barracks and cavalry yard, and renamed *El Alamo* for a military company from the town of Alamo de Parras (now Viesca), in Coahuila, which occupied it for decades. But during the fall of 1835 the Mexican Army had made the enclosure into a fort, with ditches and gun emplacements. The outer walls of stone, two feet thick and twelve feet high, were strengthened with palisades and tamped earth, until the thickness at crucial points was five feet. The Alamo, said an observer, was "a strong place."

To defend this sprawling compound, the Americans had about twenty captured cannon and a prized 18-pounder (for 18-pound balls) that had been dragged up from the coast, 150 miles away, by oxen. This gun was given the place of honor, on the southwest corner, pointed at the town. The rest of the guns were, in the main, 6-pounders, 9-pounders, and 12-pounders. This was a tremendous armament for that time and place. The Americans improved the fort, building ditches and redoubts.

"In case of an attack," wrote Green Jameson, the engineer at the Alamo, "we will whip 10 to 1 with our artillery."

A false report of invasion, in mid-January, was forwarded by Neill to General Houston, who was visiting the coast to put a damper on the "Matamoros fever." Houston, before leaving the field to Fannin, sent Colonel James Bowie to San Antonio with about thirty men and the suggestion to Neill that he remove the artillery and blow up the Alamo. Neill replied that he had no teams for the purpose. Then Bowie wrote: "Colonel Neill and I have come to the solemn resolution that we will rather die in these ditches than give it up to the enemy."

An indignation meeting held by the officers at the Alamo on January 26 passed resolutions denouncing the council and its agent, Fannin, and upholding Houston, Governor Smith, and independence. Smith threatened to have the council arrested and sent to San Antonio for trial on a treason charge. The council, no doubt frightened, responded with an order for Neill: he was "required to put the place in the best possible state for defence, with assurances that every possible effort is making to strengthen, supply and provision the garrison, and in no case to abandon or surrender the place unless in the last extremity."

At the same time, an order was issued that no more men were to be sent to San Antonio. Nor were any supplies ever sent there.

But Governor Smith had already ordered Colonel William Barret Travis to San Antonio, where he arrived about the second week of February with twenty-six men of the Regular Texas Army. On February 11, Neill took leave, on account of sickness in his family, asking Travis to accept the command. Some of the volunteers chose Bowie instead. Much has been made of the ensuing "quarrel," but it was over in twenty-four hours.

Bowie was a sick man, in the last stages of a disease later diagnosed as consumption. He was also a sad man. He had married Ursula Veramendi, daughter of the vice-governor of Coahuila-Texas, and she, together with their two children, had died of cholera in 1833.

At San Antonio on one occasion he got "roaring drunk," released prisoners from the calaboose, marched his men on Main Plaza, and generally raised a ruckus.

Travis was a handsome six-footer, ruddy and blond, hardly more than a boy. He had taken part in every vigorous action against "the despotic rule of the usurping military" (as he called it) since 1832, and now, from San Antonio, he too wrote the governor asking for money, clothing, provisions, and men. "We have not more than 150 men here, and they are in a very disorganized state. Yet we are determined to sustain this Frontier Post as long as there is a man left, because we consider death preferable to disgrace. Should we receive no reinforcements, I am determined to defend it to the last, and should Bexar fall, your friend will be buried beneath its ruins."

Among the 150, Travis counted David Crockett and his twelve "Tennessee boys," who arrived about February 10. Few if any of these were rude backwoodsmen. Among the twelve were several lawyers, while among the whole force who went into the Alamo there were at least four doctors. Most of the men were young, but it seems they were not unlettered.

Crockett climbed on a goods box in front of a store on Main Plaza and made a speech. He spun some yarns to warm up the crowd, then declared he had enlisted in the "common effort for the common cause," and wanted to be only "a kind of high private."

The ragged men at the Alamo had only beef and

CONTINUED ON PAGE 90

Looking strangely orderly, almost peaceful, with dun hills for a sombre background, the Battle of the Alamo was depicted thus in a painting made in 1885 by the French-born Texas artist, Theodore Gentilz. The attack is shown before the assailants broke through the inner walls of the citadel.

33

Father of the Modern Submarine

Dauntless John Holland not only perfected
the undersea boat but fought to get it accepted.
Both achievements brought him only grief

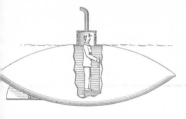

"Without celebration,"
the *New York Times* re-
ported under date line of
May 17, 1897, "the *Hol-
land*, the little cigar-
shaped vessel owned by her inventor, which may or may
not play an important part in the building of the navies
of the world in the years to come, was launched from
Lewis Nixon's shipyard this morning." John Philip Holland, her designer, hurried up to the launching platform at the last minute as the builder's wife, dressed in
a smart brown tailor-made gown, nervously held a bottle of champagne tied with the national colors. The
launch captain yelled, "Wedge up!" and then, "Saw
away!" Mrs. Nixon took accurate aim with her bottle;
and amid the cracking of timbers, the clanging of bells,
and the hooting of whistles, the first submarine to be
accepted by the United States Navy slid down the ways
and hit the water, floating "trim and true to her estimated water line."

True, nearly three years of testing, alterations, and
plain stubborn persistence on Holland's part were necessary before the Navy finally accepted his submarine.
It is a question whether he is to be honored more for
his engineering genius in perfecting the submarine or
for his tirelessness in promoting it. But the fence-sitting
caution of the *Times* proved unwarranted. The success-

*Natty, unruffled, and unbegrimed, the inventor emerges from
the* Holland's *conning tower. When the boat made her first
appearance in 1898, a Navy tug stood warily by, lest Holland try to sink a Spanish battleship in New York Harbor.*

ful *Holland* was indeed to play a decisive role in this
country's Navy, and its basic principles were to be
adopted in the submarines of England, Germany, Russia, and Japan. An even more impressive proof of the
inventor's genius is to be found today at Groton, Connecticut, where the atomic submarines of *Skipjack* design are openly compared to the original *Holland*.
John Holland, generally called the "Father of the
Modern Submarine," richly deserves the title.

The genes which determine a man's physiognomy
and the mysterious forces that shape his role in history sometimes work in perfect harmony. No one seeing John Holland's bowlered head emerge from the
conning tower of one of his submarines could doubt
this was an inventor. He was a small, intent-looking
man with rimless glasses and a bustling manner, and
his speech—direct and to the point—revealed an eager,
inquiring mind. He was, a reporter once noted,
"Irish from the just apparent bald spot above his cere-
bellum to the tips of his sturdy shoes, and his intona-
tion . . . is that of the educated Celt."

He was born in 1840 (authorities differ on the year)
in western Ireland, near where the river Shannon flows
to meet the sea. He was a resident of Cork when
in 1862 the battle between the *Monitor* and the *Mer-
rimac* served notice to the world that the day of the
wooden warship had passed. Realizing that England
would soon have an iron fleet second to none, Holland,
ever an Irish patriot, began to wonder "how she could
be retarded in her designs upon the other peoples of
the world." He began planning a submarine, and before emigrating to the United States in 1872, he had

Holland's Chief Rival

Simon Lake, inventor of the submarine Argonaut.

The Argonaut, *launched in 1897 for commercial use, had wheels and a diver's compartment to facilitate underwater exploration and salvage.*

Lake's submarine at sea. It submerged on a level keel, not bow first, as Holland's boats did.

already worked out the basic operating principles.

Holland's education had been elementary, but through his own efforts he became a capable draftsman and a fine, if intuitive, engineer. And he could not keep away from submarines. Arriving in Boston to live with relatives, he slipped on the ice one day and broke his leg; the enforced idleness gave him a chance to review his earlier submarine plans.

He was already familiar, of course, with the work of previous American designers like David Bushnell, whose tubby, hand-operated *Turtle* had very nearly succeeded in sinking British ships during the Revolu-

tion, and Robert Fulton, whose crank-operated *Nautilus* had been tested during the Napoleonic wars. And he definitely knew at least something of the gallant but tragic little *Hunley*, also propelled by a crank, which was developed by the Confederates during the Civil War and became the first submarine to sink an enemy ship of war (*see* "The Submarine That Wouldn't Come Up," AMERICAN HERITAGE, April, 1958).

In 1873, established as a teacher at St. John's Parochial School in Paterson, New Jersey, Holland was still talking submarines. Two years later a friend persuaded him to send a plan for a little one-man boat to Secretary of the Navy George M. Robeson, who referred it to Captain Edward Simpson at the Torpedo Station in Newport, Rhode Island.

The result was the first of many rebuffs John Holland was to suffer at the hands of unimaginative Navy officials. You couldn't get a man to go down in such a boat, Simpson told him; and it couldn't be steered while submerged. Drily, Holland remarked that evidently Captain Simpson "had no notion of the possibility of steering by compass under water." But to Simpson's clinching argument, that "it was very uphill work to put anything through in Washington," the young inventor had no answer; indeed he was to discover over the next thirty years that this was a gross understatement. Rejected by the government, Holland turned to a less reputable source of backing: the American members of the Fenian society, the Irish Republican Brotherhood.

United by "the strong tie of bearing one common wrong"—English rule over Ireland—these Irish-American zealots gave generously from their tiny savings to free their mother country. They set up in the United States—on paper at least—an Irish republic with its own president and secretary of war. And in 1866 they achieved their high-water mark: an invasion of British Canada by Irish-Americans, most of them veterans of the Civil War. It failed ingloriously, but the spirit behind it lingered on. Years later Mr. Dooley remarked: "Be hivins, if Ireland could be freed [by] a picnic, it'd not on'y be free to-day, but an impire, begorra."

But the Fenians were not quite reduced to picnics yet. In the early 1870's a number of their leaders in Ireland, among them Jeremiah O'Donovan Rossa, were released from jail by the English and made their way to the United States. In 1876 an American Fenian convention voted to create a "skirmishing fund," administered by O'Donovan Rossa, to finance a campaign of terrorism against England. Holland was no Fenian, but he wanted to build a submarine, and the obviously complementary nature of their respective fanaticisms threw him and the Fenians together. Not long after his rebuff by the Navy, the inventor constructed a thirty-inch model of an undersea boat propelled by a spring and a clockwork mechanism. A demonstration was arranged at Coney Island for Fenian representatives, and when the tiny model did all the things Holland had claimed it would, they set aside $6,000 from their skirmishing fund to build what was to become, under the simple title "Boat No. 1," John Holland's first working submarine.

Amid many a heated argument, Holland and William Dunkerley, a friend and fellow engineer, worked out the plans at a blackboard in St. John's School, started construction in New York, and launched her in the Passaic River at Paterson in 1878. She was a strange-looking craft resembling nothing so much as a sea-going tank. Intended merely as a working model for a larger boat, she was only fourteen feet long, tapered to a point at both ends.

Dunkerley and Holland had the little boat hauled to the Passaic River on a wagon pulled by sixteen stallions borrowed from a locomotive works. They arrived to find both banks of the river crowded with workers from Paterson's silk mills—all curious and all in a holiday mood.

Loud cheers broke out as the wagon backed down to the water, and Dunkerley and another helper, John Lister, leaped forward to untie the ropes and chains that held the boat fast. But the wagon had stuck in the mud, and when the lashings were loosened, the submarine tipped over abruptly, her nose in the water, her stern high in the air over the tail gate.

It was a bad omen, and there was worse to come. Wrestling and sweating, Dunkerley and Lister finally righted the boat and committed her to the placid waters above Falls Bridge. The mill hands cheered. And then, without warning and with no one aboard, Boat No. 1 sank slowly out of sight! Someone had neglected to insert two screw plugs in the floor of the main compartment, and the waters of the river leaked in. The cheers turned to jeers.

Once raised, pumped out, and refloated, however, Boat No. 1 performed passably. Holland found she would dive fairly well, though he made a mental note to move the diving planes farther aft and to improve the water-ballast system. "As soon as the boat came up," Dunkerley later reported,

the turret opened and Holland bobbed up smiling. He repeated his dive several times, and then he invited us to try it, but we preferred to "stick to the ropes." About the third trip we made up the river a stranger was seen hiding behind the rocks on the river road. He had a powerful field glass, and it was said that he was an agent of the British Government. His presence caused a commotion for a time.

O'Donovan Rossa and two other Fenians there for the

Boat No. 1 was a fourteen-foot, one-man vessel launched in 1878 with money from the Fenians.

Fenians also financed the thirty-one-foot Fenian Ram, launched in 1881 as a "terrible engine of war" against Britain. It was never used.

The U.S. Navy ordered the 84-foot Plunger. She was launched in 1897, but failed Navy tests.

test were duly impressed—as much by the delicious air of conspiracy, perhaps, as by the boat itself. At any rate, the experimental craft, having served her purpose, was carefully stripped of all usable equipment and the shell scuttled near Falls Bridge. The Fenians came up with some more money for a larger boat "suitable for use in war."

It had to be large enough for three men but small enough to be carried aboard a regular steamer, for someone in the movement had devised a novel plan for its use. Several miniature subs would be built and smuggled aboard a conventional-looking freighter, there to be stored in a special watertight compartment. The freighter would take them to a harbor where a number of British warships lay at anchor, the submarines would sail out through a sea door below the freighter's water line to wreak havoc among the unsuspecting men-of-war, and then return to the "mother ship."

It is not known whether Holland subscribed to this far-fetched scheme, but his second submarine was financed by Fenian money and was laid down at the Delamater Iron Works in New York City; after many delays she finally took to the waters of the Hudson River in May of 1881. Holland's connection with the Irish patriots was well known by this time (though he himself would admit nothing), and a nosy reporter for the New York *Sun* gave her the only name by which she was ever known: the *Fenian Ram.*

She was a beautiful craft, surely one of the first practical submarines of the modern type. Thirty-one feet long and powered by the twin pistons of a Brayton internal combustion engine, she was equipped for offense with an "air gun"—a bow torpedo tube operated by compressed air. The submarine could fire a projectile when awash or submerged. On the surface the *Ram* would do nine miles an hour; submerged, about seven. The first submarine to employ successfully effective diving rudder action, she underwent her first trials near Jersey City in June, when she submerged to a depth of fourteen feet. Holland himself was at the controls, and he later described his sensations on sinking beneath the waves:

Almost immediately the boat began to settle, giving us the suggestion of slowly descending in an elevator. I now looked through the ports in the superstructure and observed that the bow had entirely disappeared and the water was within a few inches of the glass. A second or two later everything grew dark and we were entirely submerged, and nothing could be seen through the ports excepting a dark-green blur.

He surfaced and returned to the dock to find a large, cheering crowd, "among whom opinion was equally divided as to whether we would ever emerge alive from our dive or not." The next day, on a bet, he took the *Ram* down and kept her down for two and a half hours, so alarming the spectators that they began to try to pull the boat up. "The man that wanted to bet was satisfied," Holland later remarked with pardonable smugness, "and badly frightened."

In her designer's estimation the *Ram* "was very successful indeed." She responded well, could "come to the surface for a few seconds to take a bearing" (Holland distrusted the periscope, which in any case had not yet been perfected), and then "dive again like a porpoise—steer a straight course in still water, and attack from a distance." She was later tested in the waters of New York Harbor, passing beneath ships and strings of barges, and at one point descending to a depth of forty feet. The air gun was successfully fired several times, using projectiles designed by Captain John Ericsson, who had built the *Monitor.*

On at least one occasion, the *Ram* gave the captain of a conventional boat the fright of his life. Cruising across the Narrows underwater one day, Holland suddenly heard the beat of steamboat paddles bearing down upon him. He dove immediately to twenty feet and headed upstream. When he thought it was safe, he surfaced and returned to the dock to find "three or four men jumping around and acting as if demented." He had, he was told, "frightened the devil" out of the steamer's skipper. The submarine's propeller, when Holland dove, had thrown up "a great mass of water . . . just as big as, or bigger than, any whale could blow." The bewildered steamboater, uncertain of what danger lay ahead, cut his engines, drifted about apprehensively for a time, then came about, and headed straight for New York.

An air of mystery and intrigue hung about the *Fenian Ram.* The Brotherhood's interest in her could

The 53-foot Holland, *the inventor's most famous sub, was launched in May, 1897, and the following year was towed to deep water for her tests. She successfully submerged and fired torpedoes, but had to surface fre-*

hardly be concealed, and submarines, in any event, were a rarity. Public interest ran high. Her novel air gun was duly noted, and there were rumors—closer to the truth than their authors guessed—that the *Ram*'s size had been dictated by the need to transport her in railroad boxcars or on the decks of ships. But by the early 1880's, after Holland's boat had been subjected to every test and passed them all, the organization that had sponsored her began once more to disintegrate, and she became the innocent victim of the intramural bickering.

One dark night in 1883 a group of disgruntled Fenians, using a pass forged with Holland's signature, stole the boat from her New Jersey mooring place and towed her up Long Island Sound to New Haven, Connecticut, along with a smaller, 16-foot experimental craft built in Jersey City in 1882. The smaller boat sank in 110 feet of water during the passage, but the *Ram* finally reached New Haven. There the Fenians made several attempts to operate her, but, in Holland's words, "handled the boat so awkwardly that the harbor master decided that she constituted 'a menace to navigation' and demanded a bond if further trials were to be made." The amateur submariners hauled the *Ram* out of the water, concealed her on the grounds of a brass factory owned by one of their comrades, and there abandoned her. "I never bothered again with my backers," Holland said, "nor they with me."

Holland had had enough of the Fenians. With the partnership dissolved, he went to work as a draftsman for the Pneumatic Gun Company in New York, and as usual began talking about submarines—so persuasively that he managed to enlist the help of his employers in setting up the Nautilus Submarine Boat Company. The new organization was reinforced, some time later, by additional backers brought in by Lieutenant Edward Zalinski, an artillery officer well known as an inventor of military devices.

In 1886, at Fort Lafayette near New York City, where Zalinski was stationed, Holland proceeded to build his third submarine. He went to work—behind a canvas screen to keep out the curious—on a "rough experimental vessel, wooden sheathing under iron frame," designed to show the stockholders that his ideas would work. The "Zalinski boat," as it came to be called, was about forty feet long, powered by a secondhand Brayton engine, and armed with Zalinski's new "dynamite gun" (which by compressed air hurled a heavy charge of dynamite a considerable distance). But when she was completed, disaster struck: the ways collapsed just as the boat started toward the water. She was almost a complete loss. In Holland's reaction, recorded some years later, is a fleeting insight into the long, lonely struggle he was to wage all his life: the accident set back the development of the submarine at least ten years, he said, "as it was that long before I was able to secure backing to construct another boat."

Holland was about ready to give up. But his work had attracted the attention of a group of young naval ordnance officers, one of whom was to become Holland's life-long friend and advocate. Lieutenant (later Rear Admiral) William W. Kimball had seen Holland's 1875 design—the one he had sent to Secretary Robeson—and knew "in a general way" about the *Fenian Ram*. After meeting the inventor in 1883, Kimball not only urged the Navy to hire him, but also gave the submarine question "a little fillip in the Navy Department."

The time was propitious, for the United States, like other major powers, was just beginning to build up a modern fleet. In 1887 Kimball and his friends managed to persuade Secretary of the Navy William C. Whitney, a zealous advocate of naval expansion, to divert some of his funds from capital ships to submarines. Open design competitions were held in 1888 and 1889, and Holland won both over some of the leading submarine designers of the day—Sweden's T. V. Nordenfeldt, for example, and the American inventor Pro-

CONTINUED ON PAGE 94

quently for bearings, the periscope not yet having been perfected. Accepted in 1900, she spent ten years training submariners before being retired. In 1917 horses hauled her to a park in New York.

Braddock's Alumni

DRAWN FROM FACT AND FANCY FOR AMERICAN HERITAGE BY N. M. BODECKER

Or, a dogged attempt to assemble a most remarkable company—the famous survivors of the battle lost by a British general on the Monongahela. Everybody who was anybody was there, from George Washington to Daniel Boone. Everybody, that is, but B. Gratz Brown

On the evening of Washington's Birthday last, my wife and I went to the Historical Society of Western Pennsylvania to hear a talk on "Pennsylvania—A State Neglected in Our Country's History."

After the lecture the ladies of the society served coffee and small sandwiches in the basement. There I chanced to see Mr. G., president of the Pittsburgh company I work for. I approached him and said:

"There is a little-recognized fact of history which never ceases to astonish me.

"I refer to the large number of men who were present at the defeat of General Edward Braddock's army in 1755 and who later became prominent, important, and even famous figures. I think I am safe in asserting that there is nothing else in history to compare with this strange circumstance."

"Indeed?" said Mr. G.

"This defeat was one of the worst in British history. It laid open the American frontier to attack by the French, Canadians, and Indians, even to within fifty miles of Baltimore. Fewer than a thousand of Braddock's men survived. But among these survivors were more than a score of men who went on to achieve personal distinction and a place in history."

"Name two," said Mr. G.

Unfortunately, the names failed to come.

"Well," I said boldly, "Colonel George Washington was there. And Anthony Wayne."

"Young man, if Anthony Wayne fought at the Battle of Braddock, he did so as a child of ten."

Next morning at the office I happened to run into Mr. G. in the hall.

"You were right," I told him. "Anthony Wayne wasn't there. I looked it up."

"Thanks for telling me," Mr. G. said.

"But Daniel Boone was there," I said. "He was twenty-one years old at the time and was a teamster and blacksmith with the North Carolina contingent. Daniel Boone later became a famous pioneer, a backwoodsman, and Indian fighter."

"I know," said Mr. G.

"Horatio Gates was there. Captain Gates was twenty-seven years old, a professional British soldier. He was severely wounded in the battle.

"Later on, Gates became a general in the Continental Army in command of the Northern Department. He defeated Burgoyne at Saratoga in 1778."

"Seventy-seven," Mr. G. said.

"There was a conspiracy, of which he was aware, to have Gates replace Washington as commander in chief. Did you know he was named for his godfather, Horace Walpole?"

"If I ever knew it, I'd forgotten it."

"Thomas Gage was also there," I said, following Mr. G. down the hall. "Lieutenant Colonel Gage was a thirty-four-year-old professional soldier who had fought the Scots at Culloden. He was in command of the four hundred men who made up Braddock's advance, and was wounded. Do you know what happened to Gage in later life?"

"I think I do."

I felt he would want me to refresh his memory with the information I had obtained the night before, so I continued.

"Gage became commander in chief of the Royal Forces in North America. On the night of April 18, 1775, he started the American Revolution by sending an expedition to Concord and Lexington to destroy military stores collected by the colonists."

"Very interesting," Mr. G. said.

A few days later, on the way to lunch, I chanced to meet Mr. G. in the lobby of our building.

"How many this time?" he asked.

"Three more," I said. "Lieutenant Henry Gladwin was there. He was wounded. Eight years later, as the major in command, he foiled the plot by Chief Pontiac to seize the fort at Detroit. With a small garrison, Gladwin defended Detroit heroically through a six-month siege.

"Gladwin was made deputy adjutant general in 1764 and a major general in 1782. He declined to serve against the colonies in the Revolution."

"You've been cramming," said Mr. G.

"Christopher Gist was there. Captain Gist, forty-nine, was Braddock's chief guide. He had been hired earlier by the Ohio Company to survey their western lands. When he traveled with Washington in 1753 to warn the French away from western Pennsylvania, he saved Washington's life once, perhaps twice. He surrendered with Washington's little army after the nine-hour battle at Fort Necessity in 1754, and he was with General Forbes and Washington in 1758 when Fort Duquesne finally fell to the British. You probably recall what finally happened to Gist."

"Well . . . ," Mr. G. began, but he obviously needed some help.

"Gist became Indian Agent for the South, but in 1759, returning from a mission to win support of the Cherokee Indians for the British, he died of smallpox.

"James Craik was not only at the battle," I continued, "but was the man who treated General Braddock's wound on the field. During the Revolution Dr. Craik headed the Continental Medical Department. He was Washington's personal physician and close friend for many years, and he was with Washington when he died."

We had arrived at Mr. G.'s club. As he turned to enter he said, "You might look up Daniel Morgan."

CONTINUED ON PAGE 80

By ROBERT C. ALBERTS

IDYL'S BEGINNING: *Winslow Homer's* The Morning Bell *caught the spirit of the early New England mill girl: coming from a rural background—and free to return to it whenever she wished —she stepped across a footbridge into a new world, and brought to it her own sturdy virtues.*

Dusk fell over the city of Lawrence, Massachusetts, a few minutes before five o'clock on January 10, 1860. In the five-story brick textile factory owned by the Pemberton Manufacturing Company, lamps began to flicker in the ritual of "lighting-up time." The big building—nearly three hundred feet long and eighty-five wide—rumbled unceasingly with the noise of its hundreds of machines for turning cotton into cloth: its scutchers and spreaders, carders, drawing frames and speeders; its warpers and dressers; and its power looms for weaving the finished fabric. Inside, the noise was higher-pitched, a relentless squeak, clatter, and whirr from the belt-and-shaft system that transmitted water power to the machinery. Some six or seven hundred "hands," mostly women, were at work that afternoon. Those near the windows could look through the twilight at the factory yard, with its two lower buildings running out at right angles from the ends of the main plant. Next to the yard lay the canal which carried the waters of the Mer-

rimack River to the giant water wheels, and beyond that was a row of frame boardinghouses for the employees. Sometime after seven o'clock, bells would jangle and the workers would stream across footbridges over the canal, home to dinner.

But not that night. Suddenly there was a sharp rattle, and then a prolonged, deafening crash. A section of the building's brick wall seemed to bulge out and explode, and then, literally in seconds, the Pemberton Mill collapsed. Tons of machinery crashed down through crumpling floors, dragging trapped, screaming victims along in their downward path. At a few minutes after five, the factory was a heap of twisted iron, splintered beams, pulverized bricks, and agonized, imprisoned human flesh.

Bonfires, lit to aid rescue workers, made pockets of brightness in the gathering night. But the darkness was merciful, hiding sights of unforgettable horror. Girls and men were carried out on stretchers, with arms and legs torn from their bodies, faces crushed

THE WORKING LADIES OF LOWELL

By BERNARD A. WEISBERGER

IDYL'S END: *The collapse of the shoddily built Pemberton Mill at nearby Lawrence, Massachusetts, symbolized the end of utopias like Lowell; the dream had been shattered.*

beyond recognition, open wounds in which the bones showed through a paste of dried blood, brick dust, and shredded clothing. The worst was yet to come, however. At about 9:30 P.M., the moans of pain, delirium, and cold coming from those still pinned in the wreckage changed to screams of panic. Someone scrambling through the ruins had upset an oil lantern. Flames raced through the oil-soaked wood and cotton waste, drove back doctors, rescue crews, and spectators (many of them relatives of the mill workers), and snuffed out the final shrieks. Next morning saw only a black and smoking mass of "brick, mortar and human bones . . . promiscuously mingled" at the scene of the tragedy.

There were ninety dead—fourteen of them unidentifiable or never found—and a long list of crippled and hospitalized. The casualty list read like a cross section of New England's labor force. There were Yankee girls like Mary York, of Brighton, Maine, and men like Ira Locke, of Derry, New Hampshire. But there were also Nancy Connelly and Bridget Doyle and Kate Harridy,

and many others whose names were of Ireland's "ould sod." There were men like the Swiss George Kradolfer, the German Henry Bakeman, and the Scotch-Irish Robert Hayer, who had come a long way to suffer at the edge of a New England canal. And there was not a church in Lawrence—Catholic, Methodist, Baptist, Presbyterian, Congregational, Unitarian, Universalist, Episcopalian—that did not have parishioners to mourn or to console on the Sunday after the accident.

What had gone wrong? A lengthy coroner's inquest did a certain amount of hedging, but certain unpleasant facts emerged. During the factory's construction, in 1853, cast-iron pillars supporting the floor beams had been shown to be cheap and brittle. They went in nevertheless. Extra machinery had been crowded into the upper floors, ignoring already questionable load limits. Brick walls had not been sufficiently reinforced against the outward thrust of those overburdened floors. After the disaster, the ministers of Lawrence spoke sermons on God's inscrutable wrath, but it was

43

SUFFOLK MERRIMACK CORPORATION BOOTT CORPORATION

clear that human oversight and corner-cutting on expenses bore much of the blame.

This seemed to point the finger at the owners, David Nevins and George Howe, who had bought the factory from its first owners in 1857, during a financial panic. Yet neither man was callous or dishonest. Both undoubtedly shared the shocked dismay of their fellow businessmen in the New England Society for the Promotion of Manufactures and the Mechanic Arts, who, ironically, had scheduled a dinner in Boston for that dreadful January 10. Nevins and Howe had acted in response to pressures which they themselves did not fully understand, and such guilt as they bore was partly the guilt of the generation of men who had brought industry to New England's hills forty years before. Those men had nursed lordly dreams of progress and profit through the machine, and some of their visions of growth and gain and uplift had been realized. But industrialism, as America was to learn, brought pain and perplexity with it as well. The horror at the Pemberton Mills was a symbol of another collapse: that of an experiment in creating a strifeless industrial society showering blessings alike on workers and capitalists. Like most such experiments, it expected too much of human nature and counted too little on the unforeseen. For a time, however, it gave a thrill of promise. Its beginnings went back beyond Lawrence, to the early days of the Republic.

In the years just after 1789, the "establishment of manufactures" was a focus of debate. Men like Alexander Hamilton and Tench Coxe looked upon the few domestic workshops of the infant nation and found them good. They urged that the national government should protect and nurture these producers of "American" clothing, gunpowder, rope, paper, rum, iron, leather, and a miscellany of other articles. From other quarters, however, came warnings that liberty and industry made poor partners. Thomas Jefferson was only one among many to point to England's experience and predict that factory workers would inexorably sink into pauperism. They would be forced by the workings of human nature and economic law to "the maximum

of labor which the construction of the human body can endure, & to the minimum of food . . . which will preserve it in life." Malthus, Marx, and Ricardo together could not have put it more grimly. Jefferson's implication needed no spelling out—plainly, an impoverished (and therefore vice-ridden and ignorant) laboring class would be indigestible in a democratic republic.

By and large, the Jeffersonians had the better of the argument for some twenty-five years. Capital, markets, and skilled labor—all necessary to a manufacturing economy—were scarce in an undeveloped America, which still found adequate rewards for its work in the soil, the ocean, and the forest. There were a few significant experiments in industry. In Rhode Island, by way of example, two farsighted Quaker merchants, Moses Brown and William Almy, set up in 1790 a "factory" for spinning cotton yarn and thread. They used many of the new machines developed in England during the preceding fifty years to mechanize the spinning process. (The British jealously guarded against the export of those machines or plans for them, but Almy and Brown found a young immigrant from England named Samuel Slater. Slater had stored away the details of the new devices in an incredible memory and come to the United States precisely in the hope of finding sponsors like Almy and Brown. He built their first plant "by heart" and made his fortune and theirs as planned. [See "Father of Our Factory System," AMERICAN HERITAGE, April, 1958.])

Almy and Brown had their new machinery tended by the children of families whom they induced to settle in the factory neighborhood, and they paid their workers, sometimes, in store orders for Almy and Brown merchandise. Thus high-mindedly did they plant the seeds of the company town and child labor in New England soil. With the coming of the cotton gin in 1793, and with years of wartime high prices, they prospered, and even had a few imitators. Yet for all these, "industry" in any real economic sense remained all but nonexistent in the United States. The

real breakthrough came in 1812, and one of the many forces behind it was, as so often, a hunch in a gifted man's mind.

The man was Francis Cabot Lowell, member of a family which was to crowd the American hall of fame with merchants, ministers, legislators, judges, poets, soldiers, and educators. In 1812, this particular Lowell was visiting England for his health, and, like so many Yankees apparently "resting," was deep in meditation. His mind ranged over a number of diverse facts. One was that the impending war would severely shake the Lowell family importing business. Another was that "yarn factories" were not a bad substitute investment. A third was that fresh inventions in the field of power looms had opened up still newer profit opportunities in clothmaking. In Great Britain, weaving factories were at last keeping pace with the healthy output of spinning factories. Francis Lowell, thirty-six years old in 1812, synthesized these facts into a dazzling American vision. Why not put spinning and weaving machines under one roof? Why not have southern cotton delivered at one end of a factory, while from the other end bales of finished yard goods emerged to find a ready market, swept clean of British competitors by war? Power would come from New England streamlets; capital from Boston's countinghouse aristocracy. Machinery? That was a little harder, but not impossible. Lowell, an amateur mathematician and scientist, visited the factories of unsuspecting British business contacts, and gave himself a quick course in the intricate process of machine weaving, which saw cotton fibers fluffed, combed, rolled, twisted, stretched, toughened, and cross-laced, moving from winding to winding and machine to machine in a complex and brilliantly-timed ballet of rollers, spindles, and flyers. Returning home to Boston, he took Paul Moody, a talented Massachusetts mechanic, into his confidence. The two of them perspired over drawings, imported a few devices, copied, redesigned, invented where they had to—and had their factory set up in Waltham, near Boston, by 1815. Meanwhile, Lowell's brother-in-law, Patrick Tracy Jackson, had helped to round up the

By 1835, only a dozen years after the Merrimack Company put up the first factory there (second from left), the five other mills shown on these pages were also humming away at Lowell, turning a hamlet of 200 into a sprawling and still-growing city of 17,000. These engravings decorated the borders of a map of Lowell and its environs published in 1850.

initial capital, and its donors had been incorporated in 1813 as the Boston Manufacturing Company.

Power, capital, machinery—all were ready. But what of labor? The more complex weaving machinery could not be run by children, and yet the cotton factory did not demand the skill and strength of grown men for most of its jobs. Obviously women workers were the answer. New England indeed had what was then called a "fund" of "female labor" in the daughters of its rural folk. But what of that supposed indissoluble bond of union between "manufactures" on the one hand, and "vice and poverty" on the other? Would Yankee farmers send their daughters into the factories to become part of a permanent force of degraded wage workers? Clearly not! Then how would the Boston Manufacturing Company recruit its labor? The answer was an invention as intriguing as any new mechanical gadget for mass-producing cloth. One of Patrick Jackson's biographers explained it, years later.

By the erection of boarding-houses at the expense and under the control of the factory; putting at the head of them matrons of tried character, and allowing no boarders to be received except the female operatives of the mill; by stringent regulations for the government of these houses; by all these precautions, they gained the confidence of the rural population who were now no longer afraid to trust their daughters in a manufacturing town. A supply was thus obtained of respectable girls; and these, from pride of character as well as principle, have taken especial care to exclude all others.

It was soon found that an apprenticeship in a factory entailed no degradation of character, and was no impediment to a reputable connection in marriage. A factory-girl was no longer condemned to pursue that vocation for her life; she would retire, in her turn, to assume the higher and more appropriate responsibilities of her sex; and it soon came to

CONTINUED ON PAGE 83

William Cary, traveling west on the

Missouri, recorded the life and landscape

of a rapidly vanishing frontier

The "fire canoe," as the Indians called it, symbol of encroaching civilization, steams up the great river past Fort Berthold, frequently visited by Cary, while the startled Indians crowd the shores.

"What a sight it was!"

By JAMES TAYLOR FORREST

Director, Gilcrease Institute of American History and Art

For adventurous young men of the nineteenth century, there was no magnet, not even the sea, to compare with the Plains frontier. Here was the excitement of buffalo hunting, beautiful scenery, and narrow scrapes with Indians enraged at the advance of the white man. Fortunately, William de la Montagne Cary, born in 1840 in Tappan, New York, combined his sense of adventure with a talented hand both for writing and for lively, realistic, genre painting.

"Pretty near the first sketch I made got me in a mess," the self-taught Cary recalled shortly before his death in 1922. Taking the opportunity of a short refueling stop on his first trip up the Missouri River in 1861, the young artist had arranged a sitting for an Indian girl whom he saw standing near a wigwam. To add color to the scene, he placed a bright-hued blanket about her shoulders. As he did this, a nearby squaw shouted excitedly, ran to Cary, and "made several queer passes" over him.

When the whistle blew for departure, Cary returned to the river boat, but noticed frantic movement on shore. A trapper who understood the Indians' sign language informed the artist that he had just gone through a wedding ceremony with the Indian girl. Cary was horrified, but, he recalled, "Then the whistle blew again and I hopped aboard. I reasoned that if getting married was as easy as all that, divorce could be just as simple."

Not all of Cary's close calls were matrimonial. The steamboat *Chippewa*, on which Cary was traveling from Fort Union to Fort Benton in the upper Plains, blew up when a keg of alcohol caught fire and touched off the cargo of explosives. Cary and his companions jumped just in time. On the same trip, Cary's hunting party was surrounded and disarmed by unfriendly Crees, but was spared death when their guide recognized his father-in-law among the head men of the attacking Indians.

The upper Plains Cary visited and painted was mostly trading country, where the far-flung cabins of the mountain men reflected the pioneer nature of the fur industry. It was still the old frontier—the gold rush that clogged the Oregon Trail in 1849 and changed it so radically would not come to the upper Missouri country until 1862, one year after Cary's first visit.

If there was danger, there was grandeur, too. A beautiful passage in Cary's diary recalls his first sight of a buffalo stampede: ". . . the air became thick and trembled, and a buzzing and droning increased until there was a thundering noise and a trembling of the earth as a million buffalo came pouring over the hill in a mad rush towards the fort . . . What a sight it was!"

Despite the hardships and the physical dangers, the upper Missouri country fired Cary's artistic imagination, and during the next fifty years, though his home remained in New York—where at one time he shared a studio with Albert Bierstadt and George Inness—he made several trips into the Plains, filling sketchbook after sketchbook with colorful and exciting scenes of Indian and pioneer life. He drew many of the famous Plains leaders from life—including Buffalo Bill Cody,

William de la Montagne Cary, aged 21, painted this self-portrait on his 1861 journey to the upper Plains country.

Rain-in-the-Face, Custer, and Sitting Bull—and was invited by them to join many of their expeditions. His oils and sketches, most of them now preserved at the Gilcrease Institute of American History and Art in Tulsa, served as illustrations for *Harper's*, *Leslie's*, Currier & Ives, and many other publishers for almost thirty years. Thus Cary helped perpetuate the frontier symbol and preserve a fast dying chapter in the history of the West.

ILLUSTRATIONS CONTINUED ON THE FOLLOWING PAGES

Indian Life — and Death

Before painting in oil, Cary drew rough sketches such as this pencil drawing of "Black Squirrel."

An Indian warrior, with his family, roasts a dog and chunks of buffalo meat over a red-willow fire.

One of Cary's lasting contributions was his portrayal of Indian customs, those of both young and old, on the upper Plains. W. H. Schieffelin, Cary's friend and traveling companion, once wrote: "He painted as he saw things, and not as he imagined them to be . . . He depicted the Indian true to life, on the spot and in all the local color and atmosphere of his wild state." In one of his most moving canvases (above) Cary showed a widow mourning the death of her warrior husband. Each of the scaffolds, raised above the reach of predatory animals, supports one corpse, partially embalmed and wrapped in softened buffalo hides. Before the widow lie the bones of the brave's horse. The medicine bags, hung on the scaffolds, were intended to ward off evil spirits.

Shooing grasshoppers into a fire provided a delicacy that was a favorite of the Flathead tribes.

A group of lively children, sent to fetch water from a nearby river, use their dogs as beasts of burden.

The Buffalo Before the Massacres

The merciless buffalo hunts that were to end in near extinction for the hordes that roamed the West were just beginning during Cary's first visits to the upper Plains. The young artist not only painted the hunts but participated in them as well. In this painting he illustrated the constant peril the Indian hunter faced after he began to track the buffalo on horseback. George Catlin, the great frontier painter, wrote of a similar scene in which buffaloes, infuriated by painful wounds, "furiously plunged forward at the sides of their assailants' horses. Sometimes they gored the horses to death at a lunge and put their dismounted riders to flight for their lives. Some blinded horsemen, too intent on their prey amid the cloud of dust, were hemmed and wedged in amid the crowding beasts, over whose backs they were obliged to leap for security. . ."

The old, the sick, and the crippled among the buffalo were frequent targets for stalking wolf packs. Above, six unfortunate stragglers, including one calf, confront their doom as wolves prepare to attack. Ugly tales were told of wolves snapping at the tongues of prospective buffalo victims, thus preventing them from eating until, reduced by hunger, they were easily overpowered. Below, Cary portrays a classic duel between two male buffalo fighting for control of the herd. The breaking cliff under the rear hoof of the bull at left seems to give advantage to his opponent. Competition—limited to the older and heavier bulls—was keen, since control of the herd meant mastery over its cows. Right: this buffalo skull was used in an Indian ceremony to attract more buffalo to the Dakotas. The skull had its "nose in a common soup plate with water," Cary noted, to let the herds know that they would not go thirsty.

Traders
and
Trailblazers

Cary met the settlers sketched above in the Judith Basin of Montana during the summer of 1874. "We came on haymakers next day and stopped over night," he wrote in his diary, "having breakfast next morning with them. Went on to hot springs and discovered I had left my blanket with haymakers." The men carried rifles to protect both themselves and their harvest. Below is one of Cary's adventure-filled paintings, The Winter Supply Train.

A trapper loads packhorses at a lonely trading post of the earl

870's, where—despite intense conflict between their races—the Indian assembled to transact business with the white man.

These sketches, of a wagon train struggling west with its burden of hopeful passengers, and of two buckskin-clad trail leaders, are similar to many drawings Cary sent to Harper's Weekly and Leslie's.

53

Jim Buter, boatman on the northern boundary survey

Artist
on
the
Missouri

A steersman

Roustabouts on the steamer Far West

Deck hands on the Fontanelle

The Missouri River was Cary's highway to the West, and it was also a gauge of the changes that were occurring along the upper Plains. In 1874, at the invitation of Major W. J. Twining, chief engineer and astronomer for the United States Northern Boundary Commission, Cary left New York and journeyed up the Missouri on the Fontanelle to join Twining's group, then surveying the boundary between the United States and Canada (See "History Comes to the Plains," AMERICAN HERITAGE, June, 1957). Passing the place where Fort Union had stood when he made his initial trip west, he found not a trace of the former outpost except "some graves of white men killed there." Cary also noted and sketched many unfamiliar sites along the river and, traveling overland, spent several days in the burgeoning mining camps around Helena, Montana. He joined Major Twining's crew at Fort Benton, Montana, just as they were leaving on the down-river trip. Along the route Cary made many sketches, such as those at the left. It was not until 1908, however, thirty-four years after the journey, that Cary executed the painting above, The Return of the Northern Boundary Survey. By then he was firmly established in his New York studio, the color and adventure of his travels on the wide Missouri far behind.

PROFESSOR
of the
WORLD'S WONDERS

Everything interested Louis Agassiz, from tiny
fish to gigantic glaciers, and he transmitted his
enthusiasm to the students of a whole generation

By LOUISE HALL THARP

Louis Agassiz, the enthusiastic Swiss naturalist, appeared on the American scene at exactly the right time and place. The place was Boston, the time, the mid-nineteenth century. Science was beginning to challenge religious concepts long held sacred. Public attention was increasingly directed toward scientific advance and toward the study of nature. Now came Agassiz, the scientist "with the Gallic power of pleasing," to demonstrate that the physical world was full of wonders and undiscovered secrets. It was just the thing that practical, intelligent young Americans were seeking: a new frontier—a glacial theory, expeditions to Brazil, mountain peaks to scale, and ocean depths to plumb. Agassiz was eager to teach, and he found an America eager to be taught.

It was as a scientist of recognized brilliance that Agassiz came to the United States in 1846. Just under forty, he had written and published his *Recherches sur les poissons fossiles* more than ten years before. He had received a doctorate in zoology in 1829 and a medical degree in 1830. At twenty-five he was appointed lecturer and curator at the University of Neuchâtel, and during the fourteen years he was there, the small Swiss institution had become a major scientific center. By the time he left Switzerland, Agassiz had about 175 publications to his credit, including twenty books with some two thousand excellent plates. He had already formulated his revolutionary glacial hypothesis, having become infected with the idea of an ice age, a whole prehistoric continent under a sheet of ice—powerful, inexorable, carrying great jagged rocks upon its surface,

and grinding rock to pebbles and sand beneath it.

King Friedrich Wilhelm IV of Prussia, continuing his predecessor's support of Agassiz, now awarded the scientist sufficient funds to travel to America and continue his work on glaciers. Agassiz went, and with the aid of Charles Lyell, an eminent English geologist, soon obtained the esteemed Lowell lectureship at Harvard. It was his first public appearance in this country, and at once he captured the popular imagination.

"Plan of the Creation, especially in the Animal Kingdom" was the name of the series of lectures he gave for the Lowell Institute, and the scope suggested by the title was typical of the man. He demonstrated what were then new ideas concerning the great age of the earth, using his studies of marine fossils to demonstrate the long passage of time and his observations of Alpine glaciers to prove his point. Some clergymen denounced him for extending the seven days of Genesis to the eras of geological time—but there was no shorter road to fame than to be denounced in Boston.

To the over-capacity crowds that flocked to hear him in Boston and all along the eastern seaboard, Agassiz spoke with a strong foreign accent, one of the many fables about him being that he had learned just enough

So eager were students to attend Louis Agassiz's Harvard lectures in biology that some of his associates, like Ralph Waldo Emerson, thought they should "check the rush towards natural history." But the lovable Agassiz, famous for his delightful sketches (as in the photograph at right), continued to captivate audiences for another quarter of a century.

English to deliver his lectures. This was not strictly true. He never would abandon his accent, however, being too much the born showman not to realize that to Americans it was part of his charm.

Agassiz looked more like a Swiss mountaineer than the learned professor that he was. Describing his first encounter with Louis Agassiz, Longfellow wrote of "a pleasant, voluble man with a bright, beaming face." And later, after they had become close friends, Longfellow said that Agassiz had "a laugh the Puritans forgot." It was when they were both on a lecture tour and met in Charleston, South Carolina, that Thackeray described Agassiz as "a delightful *bonhommious* person, as frank and unpretending as he is learned and illustrious." In the course of his investigations of Alpine glaciers, he and his associates had climbed the Jungfrau, claiming to have been the first to do so. With boyish frankness, he boasted to his new American friends that he had scarcely ever been ill, that he could carry a man on his back "and at the same time one under each arm," and that he could "lift an anvil that the smith could not."

From the moment he set foot on American soil, Agassiz regarded his stay in the United States as an educational mission. His introduction to Harvard was the occasion for his scathing remark that the university was no better than a preparatory school in Europe and that students there acted like spoiled children. His philosophy of education, both as preached and practiced, was strikingly opposed to that generally in use. "My intention," he stated some years later, "is not, however, to impart information, but to throw the burden of study on you. If I succeed in teaching you to observe, my aim will be attained." He extended this philosophy beyond the classroom, urging it on all with whom he came in contact.

And the results were no less exciting than the philosophy. People from all walks of life wanted to show Agassiz what they had seen, what they had observed. At Nahant, just north of Boston, where Agassiz eventually had a marine laboratory, fishermen would row long distances after selling the day's catch—just to bring him some strange specimen they had found in their

Few of Agassiz's colored sketches still exist. These two views of a baby flying fish are from his papers.

MUSEUM OF COMPARATIVE ZOOLOGY, CAMBRIDGE

nets. "Come in, come in and sit down," Agassiz would exclaim, delighted with the gift. If the fish were well known to him he would tell the fisherman strange facts about it; if the specimen proved new he would share with the fisherman the thrill of scientific discovery.

Strolling one day into the classroom of a young teacher at a country academy, Agasssiz remarked that he needed fresh-laid turtle eggs in order to complete a study in embryology. The young teacher promptly promised to find some and at once began haunting a nearby lake every morning at dawn. It was on a Sunday, and there were no passenger trains, when the young man finally caught a turtle in the act of laying and stole the eggs. He flagged a freight and after many hazards arrived at Agassiz's door in Cambridge very early in the morning. In answer to his ring, down the stairs came Agassiz, still in his nightshirt, to greet the amateur scientist with enthusiastic praise. The gift of sharing enthusiasm made Louis Agassiz a hero to the young man who watched entranced as the professor dissected one of the eggs, discoursing all the while on the value of the gift. "No one," a pupil said of Agassiz, "could stand before his words and his smile."

Agassiz's gift of persuasion had been early developed in pleading with his father, a Swiss Protestant clergyman, for permission to study natural history. His father was Louis' only teacher until he was ten years old. By that time, the boy could read, speak, and write Latin, so no one objected very much if he spent part of his time catching fish in the Lake of Morat, where his home, the village of Motier, was located. The parsonage, besides having a view of the Bernese Alps, had a vineyard, an orchard, and a kitchen garden, these last being much to the point in a family that had to struggle to make ends meet. Louis kept his fish in a spring-fed pool in the garden, and they made a welcome addition to the family table. When he taught himself to dissect his catch, to mount and compare delicate bone structures, it seemed a harmless hobby. His mother thought perhaps Louis would be a doctor like her father and one of her brothers. Louis' father thought that a doctor's education would be beyond their means, however, and the youth was sent to a boarding school to learn book-keeping.

Agassiz himself never made a secret of his plans. In fact, he was so openly aware of his own potentialities that, although most people took him at his own appraisal, there would always be those who considered him conceited. At about the age of fourteen he announced that he would one day head the greatest museum of his time—the Jardin des Plantes in Paris. Once literally a garden for the raising of medicinal herbs, the Jardin contained a menagerie, galleries of collections, a library, laboratories, and a lecture hall. Europe's leading scientists, among them Baron Cuvier, founder of the science of comparative anatomy, and Baron Alexander von Humboldt, discoverer of the Humboldt Current off South America, lectured there. Agassiz's father told him severely that he must prepare himself "for some humble walk in life" and not dream of such an exalted position. But Agassiz did more than dream: he went to the University of Zurich, then to Heidelberg, then to Munich, and finally to the Jardin des Plantes to study, where he became Cuvier's protégé.

On Cuvier's death, Agassiz was hired by the University of Neuchâtel in his native Switzerland at a salary of four hundred dollars a year. This princely sum enabled the young academician to marry Cécile Braun, sister of a student he had known at Heidelberg. He spent the next decade teaching and endeavoring to direct a printing and lithographing establishment which he had set up to produce his own immensely expensive monographs on European fresh-water and fossil fish. He won prizes and gradually gained a wide reputation. And during this period—almost overnight, it seemed—he became possessed by his idea that at one time the earth had been covered with ice. Baron von Humboldt, who had been his friend and patron at the Jardin des Plantes, reproached him bitterly for tossing aside his reputation as a scientist to propound so ridiculous a theory. But, after protracted argument, Humboldt came over to Agassiz's side, as did other noted European scientists.

It was then, in 1846, that King Friedrich Wilhelm sent Agassiz to the New World. In triumph his students saw him off with a torchlight parade. But the opportunity came at a time of personal disaster. His wife, who was an artist, and whose fine drawings had enhanced his first Neuchâtel publications, had given up this work to care for their three children. Depressed because she could no longer help, harassed by lack of money and by the assistants who invaded her home as nonpaying guests, she left Agassiz to return to her family. The printing establishment failed and was sold at auction. When Agassiz accepted the King of Prussia's offer, he was glad to get away. His popularity in the United States soon resulted in such high lecture fees that he was able to send money home to pay some of his debts and, as it were, to start life anew. Yet the smiling, genial face he presented to the world often hid a private sorrow.

Before his Lowell lectures began, Agassiz toured America's scientific establishments. He visited Princeton, where Professor Joseph Henry's department of physics was "remarkably rich in models of machinery and in electrical apparatus, to which the professor especially devotes himself." Of course it was of still more interest to Agassiz as a natural scientist that "in the environs of the town" of Princeton he tried—and almost succeeded—in catching "a rare kind of turtle, remarkable for . . . the length of the tail."

At Yale, Agassiz met Benjamin Silliman and decided he was "the patriarch of science in America." He admired Yale's fine collection of minerals, but again it was American wildlife that attracted him most. He had never before seen such great flocks of ducks as fluttered around the steamer after he left the train at New Haven and embarked upon Long Island Sound to complete his journey from Boston to New York. He returned to Boston to begin his lectures with his baggage augmented by a large barrel of fish he had collected in New York—at the Fulton Fish Market.

On his lecture platform, Agassiz usually set up his own portable blackboard, a roll of canvas painted black which pulled down like a window shade. He began his talks with descriptions of the most primitive sea creatures, now found in fossil form, and as he talked he drew in chalk to illustrate his words. Ernest Longfellow, son of the poet and himself an artist, said that Agassiz's sketches had the beauty of the finest Japanese drawing. "It was a real treat," he said, "to see a perfect fish or a skeleton develop under his hand with extraordinary sureness and perfect knowledge, without any hesitation or correcting." The audience always breathed a sigh of regret when Agassiz erased his work. Of course, his pictures were not always pretty. To one young lady who inquired why a certain fish was so ugly, Agassiz replied: "Oh, God must have His leetle joke."

The Swiss professor always began with "things easy to understand" and then would plunge into the more difficult, "where only technical language could be used." The faces of the "thousands of people who sat and listened would take on an expression of struggling perplexity," only to relax into comprehending smiles as the great professor made them understand.

Everyday-scenes acquired a new meaning for Agassiz's audiences as they learned to identify rocky outcroppings and to look for signs of glacial action. Wherever Agassiz went, he found something to admire, giving his lecture-goers a new sense of local pride. It seemed a distinction that Princeton's turtles should have extra-long tails. A huge rock in a farmer's pasture near Manchester, Massachusetts, once merely a nuisance, became "Agassiz Boulder," and strangers could be told how an ice floe brought it there. Agassiz's discovery of ice-scored cliffs increased the popularity of the White Mountains as a resort, and today a height near Bethlehem, New Hampshire, is called "Mount Agassiz."

By 1848, Agassiz was a widely respected and beloved scientific figure, but he still held no permanent place in American education. In that year, Abbott Lawrence, who had just given fifty thousand dollars to Harvard to establish the Lawrence Scientific School, offered Agassiz the chair of zoology and geology, with a salary of fifteen hundred dollars a year to be paid by Lawrence personally for a term of three years. To a man who had considered four hundred a year adequate, the sum was magnificent. Agassiz accepted the offer and became Harvard's first foreign-born professor.

Cambridge now found itself containing a "permanent fixture" whose personality, as well as his whole approach to education, was startlingly different from anything the town had yet encountered. At Harvard, the Boston *Transcript* reported, Agassiz "smashed all the traditions of correctness of demeanor and chilly aloofness . . . He wore a soft hat and smoked like a steam engine." His gait was often referred to as a "trot" as he crossed the Harvard Yard puffing his huge cigar. "He smoked in classroom and sent out scientific knowledge through smoke rings."

Maturity of attitude was Agassiz's first demand of his students. There were no entrance examinations at the Lawrence Scientific School. A prospective student came by to see Professor Agassiz, had a talk with him, and was told that he was free either to stay or to go. Thus, Edward Sylvester Morse, a truculent youth who had been expelled from all the schools he had attended, became a student of Agassiz's because of his extraordinary knowledge of land snails and the gleam in his eye when shells were mentioned. Morse became a famous conchologist, a professor at the Imperial University of Tokyo, and later director of the Peabody Museum in Salem, Massachusetts.

The enthusiastic teacher, realizing the limitations of nineteenth-century scholarship, never failed to caution his students that the books they read were not necessarily accurate. He put observation first, as always. Nathaniel Southgate Shaler, an early Lawrence student who was to become a professor of geology at Harvard, said Agassiz was the worst instructor but the best educator he had ever known. This would have pleased Agassiz, for it made just the point he was trying to explain to the president and fellows of Harvard: a university should be for men, not boys. Students should arrive well-instructed in the fundamentals so that they could take advantage of an opportunity for education.

It was a rule at Harvard that professors live in Cambridge, and Agassiz rented a house on Oxford Street just north of Harvard Yard. He established a startling household. Former associates from Europe, most of them penniless refugees, flocked to Oxford Street. Many were competent scientists, and Agassiz was able to find positions for them. Others were mere hangers-on who had heard that Agassiz was well paid in America and remembered his openhanded generosity. Sometimes Agassiz found himself with more than twenty nonpaying guests.

Along with the human assemblage, the house sheltered innumerable animal inmates. Everywhere he went, Agassiz continued to urge naturalists and laymen alike to send him specimens, live ones if possible. From Walden Pond, Henry David Thoreau sent fish, turtles, and a black snake. When Agassiz informed him joyfully that among the fish was an unnamed species, Thoreau was enchanted: "How wild it makes the pond and the township," he wrote in his journal, "to find a new fish in it!" In a corner of Agassiz's back yard was an eagle with clipped wings, and in a tank there were alligators. In his basement lived a bear who once got loose, managed somehow to open a keg of good German beer stored there, and then lurched up the cellar stairs—into the midst of one of Agassiz's Sunday night supper parties. Scattering students, visiting scientists, and Harvard professors right and left, the tipsy bear climbed up on the table and helped himself to dinner.

In 1848, scarcely two years after Agassiz's arrival in the United States, his wife, still in Switzerland, had died of tuberculosis. Agassiz sent for his son, but his two little girls remained for a time with relatives in Switzerland because his strange Cambridge household was not the place for them. With the thirteen-year-old Alex now added, however, Agassiz began to feel the need for some womanly assistance in managing his domestic affairs. It was Longfellow, who always took a great interest in his friends' romances, who learned some news from the French wife of one of Agassiz's scientist friends.

"It is true," said the lady, "that he plans to marry. He has need of a housekeeper." Nevertheless, it was a love match and not a marriage of convenience when, at King's Chapel in Boston on April 25, 1850, Louis Agassiz married Elizabeth Cabot Cary, daughter of one of Boston's leading bankers. "Lizzie looked lovely," her sister wrote in her journal, "dressed in a green silk,

Elizabeth Cary, Agassiz's good-natured, adventurous wife, helped found, and was later president of, Radcliffe College.

white camel's hair shawl, straw bonnet trimmed with white, and feathers on each side. After the ceremony they drove directly out of town"—to Agassiz's home in "dusty Oxford Street."

Elizabeth Agassiz received an early initiation in the sort of life that lay before her. Writing to her mother, she humorously issued a warning "to any woman who thinks of becoming the wife of a naturalist." One Sunday evening, she wrote, as she was dressing for church, "I ran to my shoe cupboard for my boots, and was just going to put my hands upon them when I caught sight of the tail of a good-sized snake, which was squirming about among the shoes. I screamed in horror to Agassiz, who was still sound asleep, that there was a serpent in my shoe-closet. 'Oh, yes,' said he sleepily, 'I brought in several in my handkerchief last night. . . . I wonder where the others are.' " When all the snakes were finally rounded up, Agassiz "had the audacity" to call upon his wife to "admire their beauty."

The deep attachment that Agassiz felt for his new home was clearly demonstrated when, in 1858, the directorship of the Jardin des Plantes and a seat in the French Senate were offered him. Here was the fulfillment of Agassiz's boyhood ambition, but he declined the offer. The Jardin des Plantes now seemed to him a trifling affair compared to the vast museum he himself planned to build and direct, with laboratories, collections, lecture halls, and public exhibition rooms. His museum was to be "a library of the works of God,"

Agassiz said, and he planned to build it in Cambridge, Massachusetts.

To realize such a vision, Agassiz would need money, but, always a successful solicitor of funds for scientific projects, he would not miss the patronage of a Bonaparte or a Friedrich Wilhelm. In America he found Francis Calley Gray of Boston, descendant of a pioneer maker of shoes in Lynn. Impressed by Agassiz, Gray left fifty thousand dollars in his will to establish a museum of natural history connected with Harvard. But Mr. Gray earmarked his money expressly for the purchase of collections, prohibiting its expenditure for brick and mortar. Agassiz now went to the Massachusetts legislature and, contrary to the expectations of his friends and advisers, got an appropriation of one hundred thousand dollars. Over seventy thousand dollars more was raised by public subscription for construction, and the first section of what would eventually become a formidable row of tall brick buildings on Oxford Street could now be started. The name decided upon was "Museum of Comparative Zoology," because Agassiz believed that the study of natural history transcended in importance the name of any one man. But the museum was soon familiarly known as "the Agassiz." It still is. A later acquisition of curious examples of German glass-blowing gave the museum its present reputation as "the place where the glass flowers are."

Agassiz found another sponsor for natural history while the Civil War was still in progress. Nathaniel Thayer, partner in the firm eventually to become Kidder, Peabody, and possessor of one of the largest fortunes acquired by any New Englander, financed Agassiz's Thayer Expedition to Brazil. It realized another early dream. Ever since his Munich days, when he had described in Latin the Brazilian fish brought back by two scientists, Spix and Martius, he had longed to go to Brazil himself to find more and rarer specimens. In 1865 he was on his way.

Mrs. Agassiz went along, the only woman in the party. What had at first been planned as a vacation for Agassiz developed into a full-scale operation, with paid assistants and student volunteers. Among the volunteers was Stephen van Rensselaer Thayer, son of Agassiz's patron, and Walter Hunnewell, blessed with a large income and an amiable disposition. Hunnewell brought along a camera and worked hard at learning the use of this remarkable contraption. Among the other students accepted was William James, future Harvard professor of psychology.

The *Colorado*, with Agassiz and his party on board, sailed from New York on March 30. Agassiz's stateroom looked like "a huge Christmas stocking into which enthusiastic Santa Clausi (or æ) were perpetually thrusting wines, cigars, oranges, apples, chocolate drops and books and newspapers," said Sam Ward, Julia Ward Howe's genial brother, who had come to see the party off. Agassiz was "flying around . . . now drawing a check, now giving an order" and distributing hand-shakes "as freely as Louis Philippe on his accession." He had been up all night, but when someone suggested he go to bed as soon as the ship cleared the Narrows, Agassiz scoffed at the idea. He must at once begin charting the temperature of the sea water "for our ap-proach to the Gulf Stream," he said.

Agassiz gave a lecture to his assistants every day aboard ship. It was a "*long* lecture," remarked William James, but Mrs. Agassiz took note of the fact that "all the passengers, several officers of the ship and the Cap-tain" came. With the optimism that never left him, Agassiz planned the exploration, "explaining over the map of South America and making projects as if he had Sherman's Army at his disposal," James said.

The expedition reached the bay of Rio de Janeiro on April 23. Agassiz immediately exerted his charm upon Dom Pedro II, Emperor of Brazil, with the result that the Amazon, not yet officially open to commerce, was opened to Agassiz, with the Emperor furnishing guides and arranging free transportation. Off went the Thayer Expedition, north along the coast, then up the Amazon in the steamer *Icamiaba*. The deck provided the "pleasantest sleeping place," and here the whole party slung their hammocks, Mrs. Agassiz's being rose-colored with white gauze curtains. "Can this be really Lizzie Cary, floating up the Amazon with a parcel of naturalists?" she wondered. Or would she wake "and find it all a dream?"

There was nothing dreamlike about the way Agassiz worked. The Amazon was teeming with fish, none of them safe from his nets. He discovered many new spe-cies, among them one that carried its young in its mouth; this he named for the Emperor, a touching tribute. Agassiz also wanted botanical specimens, and bird skins, and living animals such as a sloth, as-sorted monkeys, and some turtles. He was especially interested in the natives, but as there seemed no prac-tical way of bringing any home, he set Hunnewell to photographing them.

Some of Agassiz's happiest days were spent on a plan-tation on a lake inland from the Amazon. His artist was kept frantically busy recording the colors of lake fish new to science, while Agassiz jotted down observa-tions and plopped hundreds of specimens into preserv-ing alcohol. Here, after watching native dances one evening, Mrs. Agassiz was asked by the Indians to dem-onstrate a dance of her own people. She and "Ren" Thayer waltzed, to illustrate the folkways of Boston.

Agassiz found what he thought were glacial remains in Brazil, and would have liked to look for more in the Andes; so he was disappointed in not being able to visit Peru and Uruguay. In July, 1866, the Thayer Ex-pedition, stocked with more than eighty thousand specimens for the museum, had to return home.

Five years later, however, on a gray December after-noon in 1871, with "the first snow-storm of the New England winter" just beginning, Agassiz and his wife set out again. This time, they would explore a glacier in the Strait of Magellan, easily seen from the main channel of the strait. It had been mentioned often in the accounts of travelers, but no one had ever recorded approaching it. "A wall of ice" stretched the whole width of the valley, and Agassiz declared that this was "one of the greatest glaciers he had ever seen." Along its lower edge, where a rushing river began its course, were "deep caves of blue, transparent ice" and on going inside one, they saw "between the lower surface of the ice and the ground the accumulated mass of stones, pebbles, and boulders" called ground moraine. That night they "dined gayly," pledging the glacier in a glass of champagne and naming it, by right of explora-tion, the Hassler—in honor of their Geodetic Survey steamer.

During the Civil War, Agassiz became a naturalized American citizen. "I seem like the spoiled child of the country," he said, and he wanted to do something in return for all the happiness he had found here. When he had arrived in 1846, natural history museums were almost nonexistent. There were collections of curios here and there—skulls in Philadelphia, shells in Maine. By 1872, when he came back from the *Hassler* expedi-tion, there were good museums in almost every Amer-ican city, most of them Agassiz-inspired, many of them with Agassiz-trained curators. But Louis Agassiz could never feel that his debt to the United States was paid, and he plunged into a new project, a summer school for the teaching of marine natural history—the forerun-ner of the Marine Biological Laboratory at Woods Hole, Massachusetts.

Once more a sponsor came forward as soon as Agassiz proposed his plan. This time it was John Anderson, a New York merchant, who gave his island of Penikese in Buzzard's Bay off New Bedford, together with fifty thousand dollars, to start the project. The Anderson School of Natural History opened in July, 1873, with about fifty students, many of them women. Consider-able publicity resulted from the startling sight of "ladies dissecting fish." Agassiz's charm as a lecturer was undiminished, and workmen, in the midst of re-modeling some buildings, would put down their tools to listen to him. It was perhaps a still greater tribute when the carpenters agreed to work overtime to finish

In 1858, near Follansbee Pond in the Adirondacks, Agassiz, Ralph Waldo Emerson, William J. Stillman, and a group of learned companions found a temporary haven for observation and reflection close to nature. Stillman, the group's organizer, preserved the idyllic meeting at the "Philosophers' Camp" in the painting reproduced above. Longfellow refused to come when he heard that Emerson would carry a rifle. "Then somebody," he predicted, "will be shot." As it happened, no one was.

the lecture hall. Most of the students gathered at Penikese during the summer were teachers, and this was perhaps the most sympathetic group Agassiz ever had. It was to be his last experience as a leader in the ever-expanding field of natural science, and it was perhaps his happiest one.

Agassiz always worked at high tension and he had had several warnings of ill health, the most serious being a cerebral hemorrhage which temporarily impaired his speech and kept him in bed for many months. That was in 1869, and he had recovered. But one day in December, 1873, he went to his laboratory feeling "strangely asleep." He returned home earlier than usual and lay down on the couch in his study. Soon losing consciousness, he died December 14, at the age of sixty-six.

"Men who have made their mark in the history of science, disappear from the history of the very center where they have been most active." So said Agassiz's son, himself a scientist of high repute. But it was Louis Agassiz, the man, whom people remembered. The poets who knew him—Longfellow, Whittier, Emerson, and Lowell—all tried to express what this warmhearted human being had meant to them. Longfellow remembered him "in life's rich noon-tide, joyous, debonaire." To Whittier he was always "hopeful, trustful, full of cheer." James Russell Lowell memorialized Agassiz in more than five hundred lines, but came closest to catching the essence of the man in eleven words:

> *"His magic was not far to seek,—*
> *He was so human!"*

Louise Hall Tharp's most recent book is Adventurous Alliance, *a biography of Louis and Elizabeth Agassiz. She has also written biographies of Julia Ward Howe and Horace Mann.*

For further reading: Louis Agassiz: His Life and Correspondence, *edited by Elizabeth Cary Agassiz (Houghton Mifflin, 1885);* Life, Letters, and Works of Louis Agassiz, *by Jules Marcou (Macmillan, 1896);* Louis Agassiz: A Life in Science, *by Edward Lurie (University of Chicago Press, 1960).*

63

FROM BILLY MITCHELL'S ALBUM

In the summer of 1901, troops commanded by young First Lieutenant Billy Mitchell prepared to transport provisions and telegraphic equipment by flatboat down the Yukon River. The photograph at left was taken by him in the Canadian gold-mining town of Dawson, through which his contingent passed on its way to the Alaska border. Wrapped in netting to protect himself from the summer swarms of mosquitoes that are the persistent affliction of the Far North, Mitchell (shown below) runs the course of the telegraph line with a prismatic compass.

One of Mitchell's men (above) poses with a pair of sled dogs at an encampment on the Goodpaster River. Despite the fierce cold, work on the telegraph continued without letup throughout the winter months. With picked dog teams (right) Mitchell and a companion set out from the lonely U.S. Army outpost at Fort Egbert on a long trail-blazing expedition.

Early in his military career, the apostle of air power

blazed a trail through the wilderness, forging the last

link in a telegraph line to the edge of the Bering Sea

Billy Mitchell in Alaska

By BRIGADIER GENERAL WILLIAM MITCHELL

Few figures in American history have been surrounded by more controversy than General William Mitchell. He is a man chiefly remembered for his outspoken advocacy of air power in an age when most military minds were still firmly rooted in the earth, and for a visionary's indifference to the feelings of his more conservative superiors, which led to a sensational court-martial. Little remembered today, however, are the numerous exploits of Billy Mitchell's earlier career—among them his achievement in helping to lay the first telegraph line across the Alaska wilderness from 1901 to 1903. During his years of retirement after the famous trial in 1925, Mitchell found time to record his memories of his often incredible Alaska experiences in a book still in manuscript. AMERICAN HERITAGE is happy to present in these pages the first extensive excerpts from it ever published. The manuscript, which is now part of the collected Mitchell papers in the Library of Congress, comes to us through the courtesy of the General's daughter, Mrs. Kenneth N. Gilpin, Jr., of Boyce, Virginia.

AN AMERICAN HERITAGE ORIGINAL DOCUMENT

When vast gold deposits were discovered in Alaska at the end of the nineteenth century, thousands of fortune hunters swarmed north to stake claims. They found themselves in a land that was in turn beautiful and barren—and utterly remote from civilization. During the short summer months, communication was slow at best; in the long, cold winter, all but impossible. Early in the 1900's, however, the U.S. Signal Corps managed to lay down an underwater cable from Seattle to the Alaskan port of Valdez; but attempts to build an overland telegraph in the wild and largely unexplored territory made little progress.

In the summer of 1901, Brigadier General A. W. Greely, the famous Arctic explorer who was head of the Signal Corps, sent a promising first lieutenant named William Mitchell to investigate the delays in the Alaska line. Though only twenty-one, this adventurous son of a Wisconsin senator had already served in the Spanish-American War and the Philippine Insurrection. "Alaska attracted and interested me," Mitchell wrote, "not only because it was our last frontier, but also because it represented a stepping stone to Asia. . . . it was obvious that at some future time its strategic importance to us would be very great."

Sailing from Seattle in July, Mitchell landed at Skagway, and in the next few weeks proceeded to cover a vast stretch of territory from the Canadian Yukon District to the Bering Sea. As he traveled, Mitchell thought he saw a way to speed up the construction of the telegraph.

Until that time, he observed, the operation had been carried on only during the muddy, insect-ridden summer months; no one attempted to work in the winter for fear of the cold. But it soon became evident to Mitchell that "very little would be accomplished if we attempted to transport material through this area in the summer, as a pack horse could carry only two hundred pounds fifteen or twenty miles a day; but in winter these same animals could pull from one to two thousand pounds over the frozen snow for even greater distances. . . . Although this was one of the coldest parts of the world, it seemed to me the thing to do was to work through the winter getting the material out: the wire, insulators, poles, food supplies, and forage; then to actually construct the lines in the summer, when we could dig holes in the ground and set telegraph poles."

Greely was much pleased by the young lieutenant's findings, and late that fall Mitchell returned to Alaska. As the winter set in, he journeyed to Fort Egbert, near the town of Eagle City on the Canadian border. This lonely outpost in the gold-rich Klondike region was to be his base for the next two years. Prospects for success, however, seemed at first unlikely.

I found the garrison at Fort Egbert in rather a poor state of discipline. There were a great many recruits and few older noncommissioned officers. On account of the cold, drills were held irregularly, and little target practice was carried on. The men did not like to work on the telegraph line, or anywhere in the cold, for that matter. It is difficult to handle a group of men without giving them plenty of work, and in the North it is hard to find enough work for them to do while in garrison.

No trails existed over the mountains where the telegraph lines were to go, nor was their course definitely located, so the first thing we had to do was to survey their route. The first line would be between Eagle City and Valdez, where the submarine cable from the United States ended, a distance of almost four hundred miles through a trackless wilderness, with no means of subsistence for men or animals except game, which could only be found at certain seasons of the year.

My orders specified that all transportation in the post should be turned over for my use, and I made preparations to get my outfits out on the trail as soon as possible. I began to buy dogs to use for light sledding and reconnaissance work, selecting each one myself. The first dog I obtained was a MacKenzie husky leader called "Pointer," owned by a squaw man named Jack Lawrence, a mail carrier. My attention had first been drawn to Jack when he neglected his squaw for a week or so, to remain in Eagle City celebrating. She came up with a long knife, found where he was, grabbed him by the nape of the neck, and marched him home.

Pointer was the greatest dog I have ever seen. He weighed about 120 pounds and was perfectly sure on the trail. He could feel through the snow with his feet for an old trail and unerringly find it. We could depend on him to protect the sled and the team under all conditions. He was so fierce that we had to cut his fangs off to keep him from chewing up the other dogs. He became tremendously attached to me, and from that time on during every trip, Pointer was my constant companion and friend.

Gradually we got together wonderful teams. I selected the best ones, mated in size, gaits, and weight, and organized them into two teams. Taking a man named Emmet with me, I made a reconnaissance to see for myself where the lines should go and how we could stand the weather. When doing this advance reconnoitering, we always traveled light, often not carrying a tent but digging a hole out with a snowshoe and banking up a fire of logs opposite it, sleeping in the reflected heat of the embers. Sometimes we slept in a hole in the snow with the dogs lying on top of us.

It was necessary to push through to the south and find where the men working under Captain Burnell were located. He was supposed to work north from Valdez over Thompson's Pass in the Alaska Range of mountains, and meet me somewhere on the Tanana River, more than 150 miles from each of us.

Emmet and I sought and found the Mentasta Pass, south of the Tanana River. Just south of the pass lies Mentasta Lake, the headwaters of a small river called the Tokio, which is fed by warm springs.

We traversed the lake without much trouble, but once down the precipitous sides of the Tokio River, on whose treacherous icy surface we had to travel, we began to break through. The temperature was around 60 degrees below. There was layer upon layer of ice, with about three feet of water between them. When our moccasins and trousers were wet, they would freeze instantly and become hard as boards the minute we got out of the water. In one place I broke through with my sled, clear to my shoulders, and if my leader Pointer had not gotten a foothold on the ice beyond and pulled out Hunter, the second dog, and the rest of the team, I would probably have been there yet. Emmet avoided that hole, but broke through in another up to his waist. We were both thoroughly wet

and the dogs were incased in ice, biting at their feet to get it off. If we did not act quickly, we would be frozen to death in a few minutes.

Fortunately for us, I spied a dry tree leaning over the river, as if it had been put there by Providence. Shouting to Emmet to start chopping the tree, as he was the least wet, I drove the team ahead, breaking through the ice as I went, and began turning the dogs loose from their harness, jumping in the water meanwhile to keep from freezing stiff. I got two candles from the sled and lighted them with matches we carried in a shotgun cartridge case to keep them dry.

Emmet grabbed a double-bitted axe and went for the tree, but on raising it for the first stroke, the axe handle broke in two from brittleness caused by the intense cold. Emmet was now beginning to freeze. I told him to jump in the water while I tackled the tree. After having chopped it about half through, my axe handle broke. Things looked bad. I had a little tin of kerosene, but that had frozen. We had placed the lighted candles in a sheltered place and warmed our hands over them, because if our hands became stiff we would be unable to light the matches. I jumped back in the water, as Emmet came up with his second axe, with which he got the tree down, stripping off the branches in a second, and setting them ablaze.

In the meantime, three of his dogs had chewed through the traces and gotten loose before I had been able to let them out. But in a moment we had a roaring

MAP BY DAVID GREENSPAN

This map shows the route of the first telegraph line to span Alaska. Working out of Eagle City in the gold-rich Klondike region, Mitchell's men met the outfit moving north from Valdez in 1902; the following year they helped to complete the line to the Bering Sea.

fire, and everything was changed. Before long, I had a fine meal ready.

Within a few hours we had dried everything, repaired the harnesses where the dogs had chewed through, and prepared the dogfood of equal parts of bacon, rice, and king salmon. I always carried the best food obtainable for the dogs and fed them in individual dishes so as not to lose any of the substance in the snow and ice. Each dog was trained to come to his own dish, while I stood over them with a twenty-foot whip, ready to pounce on any animal that tried to steal his neighbor's food or make trouble.

We whittled out a couple of new axe handles from spruce wood, and started out again next morning. There was a mail station somewhere in the vicinity, and we expected to meet the mail carrier coming north from Valdez at any time. We should have met him the day before, but I figured he had been delayed. Soon I could see by the action of my lead dog that he smelled a habitation. It is remarkable how these animals show by their actions what lies ahead of them. We were running along at the base of a steep bank when I noticed ahead of us a place where a sled had evidently broken into the ice.

Peering over the bank, I could see the top of a tent. It was about lunchtime. Yelling "gee" to the leader, I jumped up the bank with the team. There in front of the tent was a sled on which a man was sitting, with his head leaning over on his hands. Sitting in front of him, immovable, was a large, black dog. I called to the man but received no response, and going closer found that he was frozen to death. The mail was in the sled under him. Between his teeth was a match, and between his knees was a box on which he had tried to scratch the match when his hands had frozen.

Pieces of harness showed where four of his dogs had bitten out and left; his only remaining companion

"There in front of the tent was a sled on which a man was sitting. . . . in front of him, immovable, was a large black dog . . . going closer [I] found that he was frozen to death."

was this half-bred dog with all four feet frozen. We put the body of the mail carrier in his tent, which we laced up, and shot his dog. Then we proceeded on down the river.

In a couple of days we arrived at Copper Center, where there was a settlement of Indians. I noticed one especially handsome large Indian with reddish hair and blue eyes. I asked him his name, and he answered, "Me named Cross River Joe."

"Who your papa?" I asked.

"Long time ago big soldier chief, he come here. He my papa," Joe replied. "Now me chief of tribe."

"Where your mama?" I went on, inspired by some curiosity.

"She live in cabin up river," he answered. I told him I would like to see his mama tomorrow, so the following day she appeared, decked out in very handsome beaded caribou-skin clothes, with a large aneroid barometer hanging around her neck, like a jewel. It was of brass, polished till it shone. The barometer had been given her as a magic talisman by the "soldier chief" who was Joe's father.

Copper Center was just north of the Coast Range, and here I encountered a sergeant from Valdez who had some telegraph supplies in his charge. Proceeding south from there, I came to the Thompson Pass in the Coast Range, where I met Captain Burnell.

I had now traversed the whole route over which the telegraph line was to run from Eagle City to the coast. We made all arrangements possible between ourselves for its completion. I returned over the trail we had broken and fortunately got by the Tokio River without breaking through again.

On this trip I fell in with the Middlefork Indians on the Forty Mile Creek, whose chief, Joseph, became one of my great friends and companions later on. He had thirteen families under him. Their country began about one hundred miles south of the Yukon and extended over to the Tanana divide. They were great hunters, trappers, and fishermen.

Every Indian tribe had its own clearly defined hunting grounds and boundaries, and each hated every other tribe. The only time they got together was in their general hate for the white man. All of them, however, respected the soldiers, especially the "soldier chiefs." I was the first officer to come into Chief Joseph's camp. As he heard my men calling me lieutenant, he always afterward addressed me as "Chief Klutina," that being his rendition of the word "lieutenant." I was later known by that name to all the Indians in that part of the country.

Back at Fort Egbert, Mitchell found his men still in a bad state. Growing restless in the dark and melan-

choly Alaska winter, they had taken to brawling with the townspeople of nearby Eagle City. Mutiny threatened. Characteristically, Mitchell decided that his best course was to get them to work as soon as possible. His plan was to head south in January, 1902, surveying the telegraph route and transporting poles and supplies to be cached along the way.

Mitchell's goal was the Tanana River, about 150 miles distant. To reach it, he took a somewhat circuitous route, following the Yukon River east a way into Canada, and then turning south along its tributary, the Forty Mile Creek, which eventually recrossed the border. "I decided to go that way," he explained, "because there was no trail broken over the mountains for horse sleighs. . . . Sledding along the rivers made the distance further but did not require anything like the exertion incident to scaling the mountains and ridges."

Progress was slow and laborious; but by the end of the winter a right of way had been cut to the Tanana. "Gradually it began to dawn on people that we were going to build the telegraph lines," Mitchell wrote with no little pride, "and that it was possible to do so in the dreaded winter. Those who had failed accused us of wasting equipment and endangering the lives of men and animals, but I never lost a man or even had one seriously frozen." Unless some unforeseen accident occurred, he felt certain that the telegraph system across Alaska would be completed within the next two years.

Gradually the streams showed signs of breaking, and we came back from the trail to Fort Egbert, putting our dogs in the corral for the summer. The snow melted from the hills and ran down, forming pools of water. From the south, ducks began to arrive, first by tens, then by hundreds and thousands. In May, the Yukon River was still frozen.

One night we heard a tremendous cracking like cannon shots. It was the ice in the river. People began yelling and discharging firearms. Next morning when I looked out, I saw that it had broken, and the river had begun moving. This is the great annual event in the North. All winter long, private bets had been laid, specifying the day, hour, and minute when the breakup would come and the ice begin moving at a certain point. A stake was erected on one bank and a tree or rock selected on the opposite side, from which a sight could be taken by two or three people, to decide when the river actually moved. Each settlement had a pool made up as to when the river would break up.

Everyone who is able to gives a party, and they visit between cabins at all hours of the day and night, drinking each other's health for the coming season.

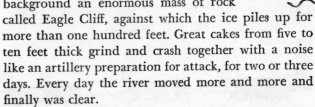

The grandeur of the breakup at Eagle City is impossible to convey by words. A great bend in the river here has as its background an enormous mass of rock called Eagle Cliff, against which the ice piles up for more than one hundred feet. Great cakes from five to ten feet thick grind and crash together with a noise like an artillery preparation for attack, for two or three days. Every day the river moved more and more and finally was clear.

One day while shooting ptarmigan on a hill near Eagle City, I suddenly came upon the body of an Indian with the whole side of his head torn off. He had a bow in one hand and a quiver of arrows on his back. Near him was a hole between some rocks on a hillside, and the snow all around was covered with blood and bear tracks. Putting buckshot into both barrels of my shotgun, I followed the bear's trail into a little open stretch of spruce timber. Within a hundred yards I came upon him, stone dead, with an arrow piercing his heart.

This is probably what had happened: the Indian saw the breath of the bear rising from his den as he prepared to come out from his winter hibernation. Going to the mouth of the cave, the Indian shot him through the heart as he emerged, then ran. But the bear, enraged at the pain, saw him, and being more active than the Indian had calculated, jumped out and happened to catch him right on the head with the first blow.

It was now the latter part of May, and instead of darkness, the days were all light. Before the snow had half gone, the mosquitoes made their appearance. Wild flowers began to cover every inch of ground.

Soon we were able to get out on the trail with saddle horses and pack mules, and get the men started digging post holes. The earth was still frozen, and we tried many methods for getting the holes down. Blasting did no good; the ground was so springy that it just bounced away and closed up again. Using steam points from a boiler was too cumbersome, because it took too much equipment to carry a boiler along and too much work to get fuel. So we used very sharp digging tools, which were sharpened and tempered every few days by blacksmiths who went from place to place with their pack mules.

Our next project was a trip from Eagle, on the Yukon, to the Tanana River, then down the Tanana to locate the mouths of the north and south tributaries of the river and determine the best place for crossing it with the telegraph lines. We were to travel by pack mule 150 miles to the Tanana, where we would build a whipsawed boat to take us down the river to Fort Gibbon. None of my acquaintances in Alaska had gone

ILLUSTRATED FOR AMERICAN HERITAGE BY MARSHALL DAVIS

down the Tanana; it was just as mysterious a country to us then as the center of Greenland or the Antarctic continent is today.

While making my arrangements, I received a telegram from the commander of the Canadian Mounted Police across the border in Dawson that Major F., my superior officer, who was on the way up the Yukon from Skagway to inspect the lines, was acting strangely, and that two plain-clothes Mounted Police had been detailed to accompany him. This seemed very odd to me, and I could not imagine what was the matter.

I went down to the wharf to meet Major F. as he came off the steamer. He greeted me with his usual cordiality. I noticed, however, that he was very nervous and kept looking all around suspiciously. Going out to my cabin at the military post, he was immediately called upon by the commander and other officers. As soon as they left, I spoke to him of the trip I was about to make, of the arrangements I had made for it, and suggested that it would be a good thing for him to accompany me, as he would get an excellent idea of the country.

Major F. said he would like to go to my office and look over all phases of our work. As soon as we were alone, he said, "I want to tell you what has happened to me recently, and then I want your candid opinion about it.

"About a month ago, I was in my room in the hotel at Juneau, when I heard two men talking in the next room. I could hear one of them saying, over and over: 'Now we have him. We will kill him tonight.' After a while, I heard my own name mentioned. I listened further and when I was sure that they were after me, I took my pistol, broke the door, and jumped into the room, intending to arrest the men and take them to the town marshal. There was nobody in the room whatever. I went out and walked around the streets. Everybody stared at me. As I passed different groups of men, they eyed me peculiarly and absolutely stopped talking.

"I went back to my room and thought it over. I thought I had better consult a doctor. I went to one, and he gave me some medicine to take, but it made my brain so inactive that I stopped it."

Here the Major paused a moment, and I asked him how he knew it made his brain inactive.

"Because I took a simple problem in integral calculus, and it was perfectly impossible for me to work it out. I was sure then that the stuff was affecting my brain. Again I heard the men talking in the next room during the night. The door of the room was open, and I rushed in, but again they avoided me. There was no one there. So I determined to come up here to you. I kept my departure a secret. Just before the steamer was to leave Juneau for Skagway, I ran down and jumped on board. As the steamer pulled out, I could see people running down to the wharf with the evident intention of getting me.

"When I arrived at Skagway, I went to the cable office and looked over the messages received that day, to see if anyone had wired ahead that I was coming and to look out for me. I found only one suspicious message which was in code. It was addressed to the Canadian Bank of Commerce. I went to the bank and asked them to let me see their cipher, so I could decode the message, which they did. It said that a shipment was being made to the bank and to look out for it. It did not say what the shipment was or anything else about it, and I drew from that, that it might mean me. I seemed to be followed everywhere, through the streets, mostly by the rougher element, who always kept their eyes on me.

"I went to White Horse on the White Pass Railway, and at that place I asked the Canadian Mounted Police authorities for an escort. Two men were detailed to accompany me, in plain-clothes, and they took the river steamer with me. A few cows were being shipped down the river, and as I looked in at them through a window, I heard the two men who were

In temperatures that sometimes reached 70 below, Mitchell made exploratory trips by dog sled for hundreds of miles.

taking care of them say, 'We'll get him before long; he is going down the river now.'

"When I arrived at Dawson, the commander of the Mounted Police met me at the wharf, and as there was another boat ready to leave, I did not go into the town but came to you right away. I saw how everybody looked at me when I got off the boat. I am sure that I am being watched and followed, and that the first opportunity will be taken to make away with me."

He stopped speaking, and I could see that my old friend was in a terribly excited state of mind. He had always been one of the bravest of men, and to see him in abject fear was a strange thing to me.

Unquestionably Major F. had lost his mind. If we confined him or restrained him physically, he would certainly go all to pieces. But if I got him out in the wilderness where he would get plenty of fresh air and exercise, I thought I might cure him. So I suggested that we start on the trip for the Tanana River the next morning.

He wanted to know if there were many Indians and if I thought they knew about the plot. I replied that there were a few, but I knew them all. They were my friends and would do more for me than for any other white man. He then asked what kind of an outfit I was going to take, and I told him one packer, four pack mules, and our saddle horses. He asked to see the packer, and I had the man, Hall by name, come in. He was a great big fellow, about six feet three in height, with blue eyes and a blond beard, as fine and straightforward in appearance as any man I have ever seen. Major F. was satisfied with him.

Next morning we got away. Major F. would look behind every tree, thinking he might find an Indian waiting to shoot him. At our first camp that night, the mosquitoes were terrible. I built smudges, around which the horses and mules stood, and put up our silk tent, which had a floor to it and a hole with a puckering string to close it up. In the middle of the night a bear or wolf came near the camp, and the horses made a lot of noise. Major F. thought the camp was attacked and made a bolt for the hole in the tent, knocking the whole thing down on top of us. Once disentangled, Major F. took a pistol in each hand and began running all around. I thought he would certainly shoot Hall and myself before I could persuade him there was nothing to be feared.

The next day we ran into a small herd of caribou. We made a careful roundabout stalk and I brought Major F. within range of a nice bull, which he killed. This pleased him greatly, not only because he was glad to make the kill, but also because he was satisfied he could hit whatever he aimed at.

For several days we journeyed on and saw nobody, but one afternoon, just as we were making camp, an Indian from the Middlefork Tribe came up. Indian-like, he approached me, gave one grunt and then sat down on his haunches to watch what was going on. After having made our camp and started the fire, I gave him a little tobacco and papers for cigarettes, and poured him a cup of tea with some sugar.

"Long time me no see you, Klutina," he said. "What for you bring stranger here?"

"He is very big soldier chief," I replied, "much bigger than me. He is chief of all the soldier chiefs in the North. All the Indians who see him must remember he is a very big soldier chief and do everything for him they can, as he likes all Indians."

Major F. had heard him say, "What for you bring stranger here?" and immediately he was off again, thinking the Indians were in league against him. For several days after this we saw nobody, and again he was becoming quiet, although he would frequently get up at night with his weapons and look around.

Arriving at our little station on the Tanana River, I ordered the two men there to whipsaw some lumber and make a boat for us to descend the Tanana River. We then proceeded south through Mentasta Pass to meet Captain Burnell's party.

In the scattered settlements of the Far North, the annual breakup of the river ice was a signal for wild revelry.

A few days later we met a large and well-appointed pack train with the supplies from Valdez. Captain Burnell had accompanied them, and we conferred again about our plans for joint action. After their hard journey, the men were certainly a tough-looking lot in their buckskin clothes, leather chaps, and long beards, their faces covered with running sores caused by mosquito bites. The mules and horses looked more like skeletons than the sleek animals one sees in the United States. I could see that Major F. was becoming nervous again. He took me aside and said he thought we had better get away from that rough crowd, as he feared he might be grabbed up by them at any moment. Here in the wilderness nobody would ever know what had happened!

We returned to the Tanana River station, where we found our boat completed, so we started down the river. For twelve days we traveled on, catching fish, both salmon and trout, and seeing many animals on the banks: bears, wolves, beaver, caribou, otter, and moose. I purposely avoided Indians on this trip, because at the mouth of the Tanana we would run into another military garrison, and I thought it best to keep the Major from seeing anyone as long as possible. He had said not a word about his hallucinations during this stage of the trip, and I thought he might be over them.

When we finally arrived at Fort Gibbon, we looked pretty tough. Our clothes were in rags. I had lost my hat in the river, and my head was shaggy. Our bearded faces were full of sores from mosquito bites, but we were in fine physical condition. The exercise and fresh air had done Major F. a great deal of good.

Upon our arrival, one of the officers began to jolly us about our appearance, and immediately Major F. was off again. He took this as an indication that the officer was linked up with the gang who were after him. His fears redoubled, and they had to send him out of Alaska under guard. Fortunately, with a year of quiet and good care, he recovered his health, and was sent back to full duty with his organization. In due course he retired from the Army, and afterward became a professor in a large university.

Leaving Major F. in safe hands, Mitchell took a steamer up the Yukon to his headquarters at Fort Egbert. When he arrived, he was elated to find the telegraph line actually working through to the Tanana River. The connection with the party coming north from the port of Valdez would soon be made. With this first line all but completed, Mitchell's next project was to lay a second one from Fort Egbert to Fort Gibbon, near the confluence of the Tanana and Yukon rivers. Somewhere along the way he was supposed to meet the party under the command of Lieutenant George Gibbs, which was working eastward from the Bering Sea.

The most obvious route for the new line would have simply followed the tortuous course of the Yukon River. But Mitchell thought he saw a shorter way to his goal, one that would save both hundreds of miles and thousands of dollars. It seemed typical of the man that this alternate route ran through a wilderness that was entirely unexplored. What Mitchell proposed was to cut a trail cross-country from Fort Egbert to a small tributary of the Tanana, the Goodpaster River. He planned to set out just after New Year's of 1903 to scout the new and hazardous route, accompanied by a packer named "Dutch" De Haus, and Chief Joseph of the Middlefork tribe, whose acquaintance he had made the winter before.

No white man had ever been down the Goodpaster River, and few Indians in our vicinity knew anything about it, because the Middlefork Indians' domain stopped at the divide at the head of the river, and the Goodpaster Indians, who live on the Tanana, did not come over on the north side of the divide. I had consulted several times with Chief Joseph of the Middlefork tribe about the trip I proposed to make down this river. I wanted him to accompany Dutch and myself, to help break the trail down there. He always said it was a terrible trip, and it was a tradition among his people that anybody who went down it in wintertime never came back.

These Indians were very bad, he explained. If they looked at you intently, they made you sick, and they stole from graves. I assured him that I could protect him against these things, that he need not worry because I had fine dogs, good toboggans that we would use on the snowshoe trails, good rifles and snowshoes, and the best of food in the North. We had become great friends, having hunted and fished a great deal together, and for that reason he agreed to go with me.

Just before Christmas I made a trip with Dutch to my various stations to see how things were going, and to make sure the men were well taken care of and would have whatever we could give them for Christmas. We had a wonderful horse trail made across the country, and with our sleds light, we went along at a great rate, often at a dead gallop. I was crossing the Forty Mile Creek on the way back, when I looked down the trail and saw a lone figure running toward me with a springy step and waving his hand. I brought the dogs to a halt, and he handed me a letter from the commander of the Mounted Police in Dawson, asking me to come there and spend Christmas with them.

We had to travel hard to get to Dawson in two days. Turning my teams in the trail, I made for the metropolis of the north. The dogs seemed to know that they were on the way to holiday and a rest. We jingled down the Forty Mile with our bells echoing from the hills on either side. That night we reached the little town of Forty Mile on the Yukon and stayed at the roadhouse, setting off early next morning.

The Yukon River trail was rough in spots, but we made good time. The winter trail along a large river follows the smooth ice as far as possible. On each side, broken fragments and high ridges of ice were heaped up where the water had pressed them aside before they froze solid. Behind them, the high and precipitous river banks thrust upward, heightening the boldness and grandeur of the scene. In some places the ice had no snow on it, and the wind whistled over the frozen surface with biting fierceness.

About three o'clock in the afternoon, the dogs showed that they smelled the town lying around the bend of the river ahead of us. We went straight down the main street at a gallop, our bells jingling merrily.

The Christmases at Dawson were renowned all over the Northland. I put up with Captain Cosby of the Mounted Police, one of the finest fellows I ever knew, while Dutch went with the noncommissioned officers, and our teams were carefully housed in a section of the Mounted Police dog corral where they could not fight the other dogs. Our teams were the envy of all the dog mushers in Dawson who gathered to inspect them.

The parties given by the various prosperous citizens were endless and all very well done. The ladies had as fine Paris gowns as could be found anywhere and wore wonderful jewels. At one dinner, we ate raw oysters on the half shell that cost one dollar apiece. I learned afterward that the shells had been brought in separately, and the oysters put on them, but they were very good indeed.

Most of the music consisted of fiddles, played by musicians who knew all the old-time dances. There were some accordions, guitars, and mandolins, and a few upright pianos.

On Christmas Eve, the Mounted Police gave a great ball. All turned out in their full-dress uniforms. As I had none with me, I wore one of Cosby's, red coat and everything else, and had just as much fun as if it had been my own.

We stayed seven days, which was plenty long enough. Had we remained longer and accepted the lavish hospitality extended to us, both the dogs and ourselves would have lost our "trail condition."

The temperature had been falling constantly, and when we left Dawson on January 2, the thermometer registered 62 degrees below zero. In weather as cold as that, when one exhales the breath, the moisture congeals instantly, and a distinct pop can be heard. It is practically impossible for wind to blow at this temperature. If it did, it would freeze you just the way a hot iron burns.

Having a long nose that protruded whenever it had a chance and was constantly being frozen on the end, I hit upon the scheme of putting a little piece of snowshoe rabbit fur on it, the hairs of which stick out about an inch and a half. The moisture from my face held it there.

Ice formed all over our parka hoods from the moisture of our breath and had to be knocked off every little while. Long beards and mustaches become instantly caked with ice, and are not only an inconvenience but a menace, as they might freeze one's face. That is why men in the North shave clean in winter, after having let their beards grow long in the summer to keep the mosquitoes off.

One often hears inexperienced men say that after it gets below 40 degrees, a further drop does not make much difference. This is not so. Forty degrees below is not particularly cold, or even 45, but for every degree below 50, the intensity of the cold seems to double.

In spite of the intense cold, we made excellent

Caribou sometimes became ensnarled in telegraph wire strung over the snow.

time, going by way of Forty Mile, and in three days I reached the head of the Middlefork River and scaled the high divide where I had ordered a cache of supplies to be made. Here I was met by Chief Joseph. He had brought an excellent outfit with him, good snowshoes, caribou-skin clothing, and a 30/30 carbine. He seemed quite melancholy, however, and told me that he might never see his own people again as he was going with me into the country of the bad Indians. Although I did not expect to encounter any very unusual conditions, I knew that a long snowshoe trip with the temperature below 60 degrees was a serious thing, particularly if we ran into any warm springs and broke through the ice. The temperature had been falling steadily. It was now under 70 degrees below zero.

We found the Goodpaster to be a beautiful stream, gradually broadening out between washed-down hills, with excellent timber. We threaded our way through groves of spruce trees, birches, and alders, and as we descended the river course, we began to get more and more into the bed of the stream.

The terrible cold continued, constantly around 70 below. The wise huskies would stop every little while and bite the snow out of their feet to keep them from freezing. A snowshoe trail in cold weather is extremely hard on dogs, because even after it has been broken, the dogs go in almost up to their bellies. As their feet go down through the snow, their toes spread out, with the web and hairs projecting so as to offer the greatest surface possible. The snow sticks to the hair between the toes, and in a little while it is a good deal the same as marbles between them.

We made about fifteen miles a day, which we considered good, as the snow was quite deep compared to the Yukon. On our fifth day out we ran across a trail which Joe at once pronounced to be made by an Indian, one of his tribe, he thought, who had left his own country and gone into the forbidden territory because it was so rich in furs. The trail went ahead of us down the river. Soon we saw the smoke of a fire rising through the spruce trees, and getting closer, saw an Indian wickiup, a lodge built something in the form of a beehive, covered with bark and spruce boughs.

"Him David house. I guess he die," said Joe, meaning that the lodge belonged to a man of his

Indian David, of the Middlefork tribe, whom Mitchell saved from starvation.

tribe named David, who was probably starving to death.

Leaving Dutch with the dogs, Joe and I went to the wickiup and looked in. There sat David with his head in his hands, emaciated and pale. Three children, practically unable to move, were on the other side of him, while his squaw was just able to put wood on the fire. Three dogs were in the lodge, two of them hardly able to move, but one came toward the door to try to attack us. He was so weak he fell into the fire on the way and had to be pulled out.

Joe talked to David and elicited the information that David had come across with his family at the first snow. It had grown cold so quickly that he had been unable to get sufficient caribou meat to last him through the winter. The snow was so light that the game ran right through it, but it offered the maximum impediment to snowshoes. He had only killed a couple of caribou since the middle of November, and for over a month they had subsisted on moosehide from their moccasins and the sinews out of their snowshoes, had eaten one dog, and were about to kill the others. All these Indians seemed perfectly numb, mentally and physically, so exhausted were they. A white man under the same conditions would have frozen and died long before.

We had been hitting a terrific gait along the trail. Dutch was getting tired, but Indian Joe was becoming much more so, although neither of them said anything about it. I therefore decided to give them a day's rest and at the same time try to save this Indian family. If I split my own meager store of provisions with them at that time, they would eat everything up in a few days; so I gave them only meals that we cooked ourselves during the day we were there, and left them just enough food to last for ten days, by which time I expected to return.

Naturally this was cutting down our own supply pretty low, but I knew I could get to the mouth of the Goodpaster in four or five days, and I expected the Indians there to have some dried salmon left and possibly some game. We chopped an additional store of wood for David's family and fixed up his lodge. The effect of a little food on the dogs was even more marked than the effect on the Indians.

The day's rest had stiffened up both Joe and Dutch, who showed increasing signs of fatigue. Dutch kept lagging behind, so I sent him forward where I could watch him. When cold begins to seize people, they become very pleasant, and everything seems rosy to them. They want to lie down and take it easy, and when they do, they freeze to death in a couple of minutes.

The second day out from the camp of the starving Indians, Dutch began to lag behind worse than ever.

As we rounded a turn in the river, I looked back and did not see him. I could tell by the action of the Indian that he was worried. A little way down the stream we saw a dry spruce tree, sticking over the bank above the ice. I told Joe to go down there and make a fire instantly while I ran back on my snowshoes to look for Dutch. I found him about 150 yards back, lying in the snow. I spoke to him, asking him why he had not kept up. Dutch answered that he was so tired he had to lie down and take a rest, and he didn't believe it was possible for him to move, that he was perfectly comfortable there in the snow.

It was a typical example of the stage where circulation begins to slow up, preparatory to freezing. I jumped squarely on his face with both my snowshoes and wiggled them around, then jumped on his chest and kicked him in the stomach, all the time abusing him verbally, trying to make him get up and fight me. At last I got him on his feet and slapped him in the face as hard as I could with my open hands, to make him so mad that he would exert himself. Dutch was a good man physically, and ordinarily would take no foolishness from anybody, but I had a terrible time trying to rouse his ire and get him started down the trail. At last I succeeded and walked along with him, hitting him every few moments and dragging him along. As we rounded the turn, I saw that Joe had gotten the fire started in a jiffy. Flame and smoke were rising from the dried spruce boughs.

The sight seemed to work a transformation in Dutch. His eyes stuck out, and he made straight for the fire. When he got there, he jumped squarely into it. We had to drag him out to keep him from burning himself. As it was, he burned a part of one snowshoe and one moccasin, and it took us an hour to repair them. He now began to tingle all over and appreciate how cold he was.

I had two bottles of Perry Davis Pain Killer in each sled. This is the greatest medicine ever invented for use in the North. I do not know the ingredients, other than alcohol and some laudanum, but I would hazard a guess at red pepper, turpentine, and tabasco juice. You can take it internally or rub it on as a liniment. For man or dog, it is one of the best remedies I know for frost bite.

I gave Dutch a good swig of it and rubbed some on his neck and chest. In a little while he was well heated up. We ate a good hearty lunch, and I filled him full of hot tea. Then I put him ahead of the sleds and kept him there for the rest of the trip.

Five days out from David's house, or ten days away from the head of the Goodpaster River, we reached its mouth, a distance of 170 miles. Rounding a point, we came all at once on the Indian village, which consisted of ten or twelve log cabins, with caches outside of them. Birchbark canoes were piled up for the winter outside the houses, and sleds and dogs were in front of the doors. As the dogs heard our bells, they put up a great hue and cry. An Alaskan dog cannot bark, it can only howl. If one does hear a bark in the North, it is an unmistakable sign that the dog is of an outside breed.

As we came up the bank to the village, these Indian dogs ran up to my leader, Pointer, apparently with the idea of biting him. Pointer grabbed one of them by the throat and threw him five or six feet, never looking at him at all, but keeping right on the trail. The dog beat a hasty retreat, and none of the others came near us again.

The Indians seemed tremendously astonished to see us, and eyed my Indian, Joe, curiously. He spoke an entirely different language from their own, but he made himself understood by signs and a few words common to all Indians. Several of the Goodpaster Indians spoke quite a few words of English, having been down to the mouth of the Tanana River to trade their furs.

I explained to them that I was a soldier chief, engaged in putting up a "talk string"—as they called the telegraph wire—which I said would be a great assistance to them when installed. One asked me if it would bring more white men into the country, and I told him it probably would not, because the "talk string" would do the work of many mail carriers who otherwise would have to go through that country. One Indian said he had heard that game would not cross the "talk string," and that therefore the migration of the caribou would be changed, much to their disadvantage.

This was really so. The caribou at first were very much afraid of the right of way that we chopped through the country and of the wire that was laid on the ground, because when they came into contact with it, it cut their legs. We found that caribou had become entangled in our wire in several places and pushed it a hundred feet away from its original location, but afterward let it severely alone. Gradually they became used to it and after a while crossed the right of way without hesitation. I explained this to the Indians and told them it would make no difference with the caribou migration. In addition, the telegraph line went straight from point to point and would always afford them a fine winter trail.

They asked me why I had brought an Indian of another tribe with me, because he might find out things there which they did not wish him to know. I replied that I was a soldier chief, and he was an Indian chief, that we were great friends and companions, hunted and fished together, and I had made him come with me against his will, to assist me on this trip.

The Indians seemed satisfied with these explanations and told me they were glad to see me, that I was the first white man who had ever come down the river, and they were greatly surprised that I came through in this terribly cold weather. They themselves had even stopped trapping, they told me.

After having provided for our dogs and eaten a good meal ourselves, we settled down to smoke, and I gleaned from the Indians all the information I could about the country. I asked when they thought the breakup would come in the spring, and where they thought was a good place for us to build boats. The conversation shifted to when the salmon would come, whether there were many of them, how much game there was in the country, and where it was located. The Goodpaster, they told me, was the best place for marten, or Alaska sable, but the Delta River, the mouth of which was about ten miles below, was the best place for foxes, particularly black and silver tips, several of which they had obtained during the last month.

Finally, an Indian who was telling me about the Delta River, said, "Me come back yesterday from line of traps, Delta River, me catchum two white men. They heap sick, too much eat."

This was astonishing information, two white men in the country at that time of the year, and sick from eating too much! I could get no more out of him except that he had left two Indians with them, that he had given them frozen salmon to eat, and that they had been on the trail a long time, coming from the Copper River. Joe elicited the information that these men were nearly frozen to death and in a very bad condition.

I determined to push down there at once and see what the trouble was. Telling one of the Goodpaster Indians to start down ahead of me, I borrowed a sled from them to use instead of my toboggan, hitched my team to it, took a little rice and bacon with me, and left Dutch to look after things at the Goodpaster village.

In a couple of hours I reached the Indian camp, a little above the mouth of the Delta. Sure enough, I found two white men, one an Irishman and the other a Swede. The Indians had built a nice wickiup for them, with a comfortable fire which made it quite warm. The Irishman's face and hands were entirely black from freezing, and his ears were all shriveled up and sloughing off. The front teeth of both men were broken off from having tried to bite into the frozen fresh salmon which the Indians had given them, and both were very sick at their stomachs from having eaten so much of it. The Swede was in much better condition than the Irishman. His toes and fingers were a little frozen, but his face, except for the nose and ears, was pretty clear of frost, as were his legs, arms, and back.

I looked over the Irishman. The Indians had taken off his trousers and were rubbing him with snow to try and save him, but I saw at once that his legs were gone and probably his arms. He had worn suspenders to hold up his trousers, and these had frozen from the moisture. There was a black streak on each side of his chest and down his back where they had extended. I did not see how the man could have lived.

I gave him a little Perry Davis Pain Killer, and cooked some rice, bacon, and salmon for them. It would have been impossible to get these men back to my working parties or to Eagle City, but there was a trading station at a little place called Chena, about a hundred miles below, where a gold strike had just been made. I therefore told the Indians that they must mush these men on down there, and they would be paid liberally for their efforts by the government or by private individuals. Both the frozen men said they had plenty of money and produced an order from the Northern Commercial Company to give them practically anything they wanted.

In the meantime, the Swede, whose vitality seemed enormous, began telling me what had happened to them. To begin with, he and his partner had determined to go into the upper Tanana River country, as they thought it offered the best chance for making a strike. During the summer they hired some packers to take them up the Chestachina River, and carried a good outfit across the divide, which is without timber for about thirty miles. They made a good strong cache for it, which would resist wolverines or any other animals, then crossed the divide and waited for the freeze

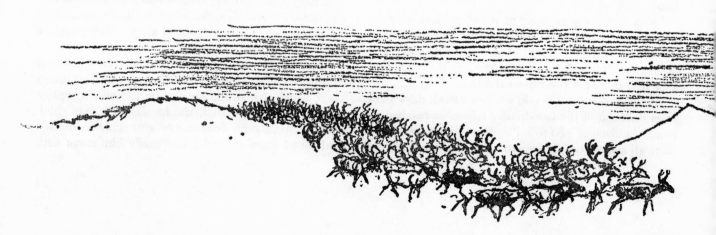

in a cabin on the Chestachina about fifty miles from their cache.

When the freeze came, they crossed the divide under great difficulty, then found that their cache had been robbed by the Delta Indians of everything except a little corn meal. They debated whether they should go back or go ahead, and decided that the trip back was almost as bad as the trip ahead. As they were both good shots, they thought they could kill game sufficient for their subsistence, but little did they know about hunting at that time of the year in northern Alaska. They saw sheep several times but could get nowhere near them, and in a week's hunting only killed two rabbits.

Still they decided to push ahead. Soon their scanty supply of corn meal was exhausted. They went several days without eating, and their dogs became so exhausted that they could go no further. A dog can work from four to seven days without anything to eat. After that he dies if he is not fed. So they killed one dog, ate some of it, and fed the rest to the other dogs. This carried them on a little further. Two dogs ran away, which left them only two others. These they also killed. Pulling their own sled, they still made from six to eight miles a day.

Eventually, the terribly cold weather overwhelmed them. Their clothing and outfit were not sufficient to stand it. The Irishman began to freeze more and more every day and could not thaw out properly. When all their dog meat was gone, they chewed the dog hides, then ate all the webbing out of their snowshoes. They ate their moccasins and attempted to make sandals for their feet out of birchbark. Finally they ate their mooschide mittens, leaving only the woolen linings to wear, which of course soon became wet and froze their hands. By that time they were nearing exhaustion and really had expected to die in the camp where the Indians found them.

I urged the Indians to make all haste to take them down the river. They did it and did it well, sending two sleds with two Indians each. I afterward found that they got the men to Chena in about four days, in as good condition as could be expected. The Swede lost only two or three fingers and the ends of a few toes. The Irishman lost both legs and both arms. I saw him several months afterward, and he remarked in a jocular way that he did not know whether it was better to be dead or alive in that condition. His face was a mass of scars and his ears practically eaten away.

Even in the dead of winter, news of Mitchell's trailblazing exploit spread quickly through the Alaska wilderness. If his new route to the Tanana River shortened the projected telegraph line, it also gave fast, though hardly easy, access from the Klondike to the newly opened Tanana gold fields near Chena and Fairbanks. At Fort Egbert, Mitchell discovered that men were already outfitting to make the trip; despite the rigors of the arctic winter, the migration of gold-seekers over the Goodpaster trail soon amounted to a stampede.

Mitchell continued to make long survey trips to the Tanana and back. During one stay at Fort Egbert, he became a member of the Society of Arctic Brothers, a secret organization of men who have spent at least one winter in the North and become "sourdoughs." His initiation called for him to walk barefoot in the snow at 35 degrees below zero. Then he was brought before a "tribunal" and accused of purposely starving his men on the trail to the Tanana. "The charge had the exact effect that they desired on me," Mitchell wrote. "I got very mad and challenged the fellows that made it to come out and fight me right there. So we went outside, and they grabbed me and rolled me around in the snow for about five minutes, then brought me in and gave me a good warm spiced drink and invested me with complete membership in the order."

As the spring of 1903 approached, Mitchell made preparations for the completion of the telegraph line. At Central, his advance base at the head of the Goodpaster, he put his men to work building boats to transport crews and equipment down the Tanana as soon as the ice broke. It was his hope that he would meet the party of Lieutenant Gibbs, which was working toward him, sometime that summer. While there was still snow on the ground, he made a final trip to Fort Egbert and Eagle City, 150 miles away. Stopping only once for a brief meal, Mitchell and his friend "Dutch" De Haus covered the distance in a little less than twenty-four hours. The two men had established a record for a single day's journey with a dog team.

I went back to Central, to find the boats practically finished. There were five quite large ones, about eighteen feet long, which would hold one ton of cargo, four rowers, and a steersman; and for my own use, a double-ender, twelve feet long. Despite their crude tools and equipment, the men had built excellent boats.

Mitchell often spent his spare hours hunting the caribou that roamed in vast herds through the Alaska wilderness.

I organized the crews and practiced them in rowing and steering. I put our best men with the two boats containing our reserve food supplies, so as to insure their getting through in good shape. They were to stop at the mouth of the Goodpaster, opposite the Indian village, and organize a camp from which supplies could be distributed up and down the river.

Shooting rapids on the Tanana River

I started the pack trains through the water while the ice was still floating on it. They carried the working parties along the line where they were to erect the poles, put on the insulators, and tie the telegraph wire on. Our wire had now been laid all along the right of way from the head of the Goodpaster to the Tanana, and it remained for me to determine the course of the line from that point on down to where we met the other party.

We had practically continuous light at this time. I started out in the lead with my boat, ordering the others to come at two-hour intervals so that if anything happened to us in front, we would have sufficient time to run upstream and signal to them what to do.

Old Dutch was at the oars in my boat, and he proved to be a pretty fair oarsman. I manned the two steering sweeps in the stern, which I used to avoid drifts, rapids, or "sweepers," that is, trees which had fallen into the water but whose roots had not been detached from the earth. They would be carried downstream by the current, then would spring back and repeat the operation. It was a very dangerous thing to get caught under one of them.

I sat in the stern, with Dutch in front of me at the rowing bench. The Goodpaster was beautiful; the trees were beginning to take on their summer aspect, and the bushes were completely clothed with bright green leaves. Wild flowers covered the ground. We were so confident now that we would finish the telegraph line that summer that we had ceased to talk about it.

That night we made camp at the mouth of the Goodpaster. I decided to wait there until the other boats arrived and reorganize the expedition. Mosquitoes were beginning to get bad. It is impossible to convey to one

who has not been in the North how terrible these insects really are. At night we built long smudges, or slow-burning fires, around which the mules and horses stood to escape the mosquitoes. After a while the animals got so they would not even leave the smudge to feed or graze, so great was the pain inflicted by the bites. Two of my mules were literally killed by mosquitoes on this expedition. They were bitten so severely that they would not leave the smudges to feed and grew constantly weaker. Later, trying to avoid the mosquitoes, they got into the swift water of the Tanana and were swept away and drowned.

Dutch and I worked down the river ahead of the working parties. When I found a suitable place to land, I would get out on the bank, strike the line where the telegraph should go, then with my prismatic compass lay a straight line from one point to another, and blaze the trail through myself, alone. I laid out from five to ten miles a day in this way. It was difficult working through the underbrush, bogs, and wet moss, with the mosquitoes and insects to contend with, but much easier and quicker than carrying a big outfit and several men along with me.

Rounding the promontory which is at the mouth of the Delta River, we entered Bates' Rapids of the Tanana. The water here was much swifter than I had supposed. The river was wide, with an interminable number of sloughs. The current ran at a prodigious rate, carrying with it whatever trees or other floating material got into it. These things lodged on the bends, bars, or on projections along the banks and made a great heap like a log jam under which the current raced and roared. If a boat got under them, it would be all off with it.

We had only about one hundred miles more to go to finish the line, so I determined to take one of the large grub boats and handle it myself, to be sure that nothing happened to it on the way down. I had one of my other men take my own boat while I took Dutch and three others, all of them at the oars, two on each side. One was an ex-constable of the Canadian Mounted Police, a very good man on the water. I stood up in the stern and had a twenty-foot sweep with which to steer the boat. The channels were crooked and in many places "sweepers" fifty feet long hung over them, going down with the water, then rising with a swish and falling again.

We made very good time, and I was able to avoid both "sweepers" and the great piles of drift on the bars. I had never before seen such swift water, nor have I since. Suddenly the channel narrowed, and the speed of the current increased. I could see there was a sharp turn ahead, on the other side of which there would be an eddy, due to the water hitting the point and then swirling on the other side. Directly opposite this point was a long "sweeper," a green spruce tree. Green trees are much more limber than dead ones, and whip in and out of the water with an incredible swing. If this "sweeper" hit us, we would certainly be swamped and lose our grub, and thus be delayed another year on the work. It was the supreme moment of test, on which hung the success of our expedition.

Shouting to the men to put on all the speed they could so as to get steerage, away we shot for the point. I planned to swing the boat as we got there, aiming it to the right and trusting it would hit the eddy on the other side and carry us to safety. As we neared the point, I thought I would make it. Standing in the stern, I pulled my steering sweep with all my might, but just as I did so, the spruce caught me squarely across the waist and lifted me from the boat.

Below us was a great pile of driftwood on a projection of the bank under which the water swirled. I knew if I let go of the tree, I would be carried under the driftwood and never be heard from again. The tree carried me under the icy water, then flopped up about fifteen feet in the air, then fell again and went under the current. I could hear Dutch telling me to hold on, and the other men shouting as they pulled for the shore. A quarter of a mile below me the boat landed. By that time I had wrapped both my arms and legs around the trunk and found that I could hold my breath while the "sweeper" went under the water. I thought I could hang on for fifteen or twenty minutes at least, but if I were swept off at the end of that time, I would have so little strength left I could not avoid going under the drift pile.

I saw three men leave the boat the instant it touched the shore, while a fourth made it fast to the trunk of a tree. One of them had a big coil of rope, another an axe. Never have I seen men work faster or to better effect. Going to the bend about thirty feet upstream from me, they tied the rope around Dutch, over his right shoulder and under his left arm, then took a turn around his body. They snubbed the rope around a tree, and Dutch jumped into the raging current, being let down gradually by the other three until he got to the point where the "sweeper" carried me upstream and down into the water. As I came up, he grabbed me around both shoulders, and I grabbed him. Holding on to each other like vises, we were pulled in by the other three men.

As we landed, Dutch said to me, "I don't know if we are even, but you saved me from freezing last winter, and I have pulled you out of a bad place in this river." If it had not been for men like these, I doubt if I would have been rescued.

We completed the trip twenty miles down the river that day without further mishap. Here we stayed several days, while I ran the course of the line up and down. Then Dutch and I took our small boat and dropped down to the mouth of the Salcha River, a few miles below. Again I ran the course of the line, meeting my men about twenty miles up the river as they worked chopping out the right of way. Never have I seen greater physical strength or endurance displayed by a group of men. There were twenty in each working party, great bearded fellows in blue denim clothing, high horsehide boots and slouch hats, with remnants of mosquito netting around the edges. Their faces were running sores from the terrible assaults of the mosquitoes and black flies. As they attacked the spruce trees, the forest seemed to fall in front of them. Without such men, the lines in the North could never have been completed.

For a couple of weeks we worked with great speed. Already our parties had gotten in touch with those of Lieutenant Gibbs working up the river. July was approaching, and now I had no doubts that we would finish the telegraph system that summer. At last my wire crossed the Salcha River. Because of lack of transportation, Gibbs had fallen a little behind in his work, and I had to extend on beyond, but at length we reached the end of his wire. I made the last connection of the Alaska system myself.

Then from St. Michael and Nome on the Bering Sea, clear through to New York and Washington, the electric current transmitted our messages with the speed of light. Alaska was at last open to civilization. No longer was it the land of the unknown, sealed tight by the God of Everlasting Snow and Frost. We had forced open the portal with which he shut out the white man from the North.

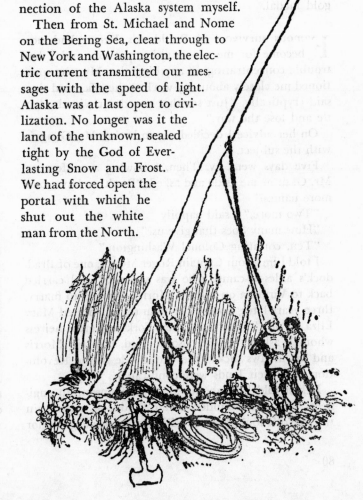

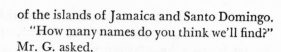

Braddock's Alumni

CONTINUED FROM PAGE 41

I continued on to meet some friends for lunch. As I approached the table I thought I heard one of them say to the others, "Here comes Old Braddock's Defeat," but I decided I was mistaken. Probably he actually said something like "This cold's bad for the feet." So I told them about Gladwin, Gist, and Craik.

Back at the office I looked up Daniel Morgan and found that Daniel Morgan had indeed been there.

Morgan, I discovered, had enlisted with his own team of horses and a wagon—an "independent wagoner," nineteen years old, six feet tall, and with a fiery Welsh temper.

In the course of the Revolution, Washington formed a regiment of five hundred of the best marksmen in the country and placed Morgan in command. In Benedict Arnold's unsuccessful assault on Quebec at the end of 1775, Morgan and his riflemen penetrated well into the city but were cut off and forced to surrender. He was freed in time to play a key part in the Battle of Saratoga. Brigadier General Morgan was in command at the decisive Battle of Cowpens, for which Congress voted him the thanks of the nation and a gold medal.

Famous survivors of Braddock's Defeat had now become for me a consuming passion, and I had trouble concentrating on anything else. My wife questioned me closely about my work at the office and then said cryptically, "Just see that you don't win the battle and lose the war."

On her advice I decided not to bother Mr. G. again with the subject.

Five days went by. Then, following a conference, Mr. G. drew me aside and asked, "Don't we have some more names?"

"Two more," I said happily.

"How many does that give us?"

"Ten, counting Colonel Washington."

I told him about Captain Roger Morris, one of Braddock's aides-de-camp, who was wounded and carried back to Virginia on a litter. Morris survived to marry, three years later, none other than the celebrated Mary Eliza ("Polly") Philipse of New York—the great heiress whom Washington had also courted. Captain Morris and his in-laws picked the wrong side in the Revolution, and their lands were confiscated.

I then told him about Adam Williamson, an engineer, who was wounded under Braddock, and again when Wolfe took Quebec. Williamson became governor of the islands of Jamaica and Santo Domingo.

"How many names do you think we'll find?" Mr. G. asked.

"I don't know. If I went about this thing seriously I think we could find as many as twenty prominent men who were there July 9. I'm going to shoot for exactly twenty and then stop."

"Well," said Mr. G., "let me know how it turns out."

I spent most of that weekend in the Carnegie Library. Monday morning I dictated the following memorandum to Mr. G.

"I beg to report that I have established indubitably that the following men were present on July 9, 1755, and achieved distinction in later life:

"George Croghan, thirty-seven, captain in charge of Braddock's friendly Indian scouts, was greatest of the Indian traders. In 1756 Sir William Johnson appointed Croghan Deputy Superintendent of Indian Affairs. During the sixteen years he held this post, he was the most important and powerful man on the frontier.

"Croghan was with Forbes at the taking of Fort Duquesne, helped Bouquet occupy Detroit in 1760, and conducted the final peace negotiations with Chief Pontiac. Owner at one time of several million acres of frontier land, he died poor. His journals are of prime historical value.

"Patrick Mackellar, second engineer of the expedition, was with Gage in the advance column and was wounded.

"Major Mackellar was captured by the French in a later engagement and imprisoned in Montreal and Quebec, where he drew engineering maps of the fortifications. He was exchanged in 1757 and sent to England, but he returned to North America, his maps in his pocket, in time to participate in the sieges of Louisbourg and Quebec. He was standing beside Wolfe when that general was killed.

"In 1762, Mackellar became chief engineer of the Island of Minorca, and later he became England's Director of Engineers.

"Ralph Burton was second in command of the 48th regiment and performed gallantly in the battle until disabled by a wound. Lieutenant Colonel Burton commanded the same regiment at the taking of Quebec four years later. General Wolfe's dying words were: 'Go, one of you, my lads, with all speed to Colonel Burton and tell him to march Webb's regiment down to the St. Charles River, and cut off the retreat of the fugitives to the bridge. Now, God be praised, I die happy.'

"Burton rose to major general in 1762. About this time, he fell madly in love with the tawny daughter of an Indian chief; some say that he married her.

"John Neville was a twenty-four-year-old private

from Virginia. In 1775, as a colonel of militia, Neville commanded Fort Pitt for two years. He was later attached to Washington's army for the duration of the war; in 1783 he was made a brigadier general.

"A Federalist and a wealthy man, Neville served as a member of the Pennsylvania Council which ratified the Federal Constitution and of the Pennsylvania Constitutional Convention.

"Now we have fourteen names and six to go."

To this communication Mr. G. replied almost at once.

"I am surprised that you have overlooked two of the most important and interesting figures of all those present.

"Captain Adam Stephen was a hot-headed Scot, twenty-five years old, a bachelor, who had served with Washington at Fort Necessity—that 'charming little spot for an encounter' which started the Seven Years' War, involved England, Prussia, Germany, Austria, and Sweden, devastated Germany, swept across India, and cost a million lives. Stephen was wounded at the Battle of the Monongahela, and later gave the widely quoted description of the British regulars standing 'in a mere huddle' under fire.

"Stephen was disinclined to obey orders and inclined to drink, gossip, and engage in factional quarrels. During the Revolution he rose to the rank of major general in the American Army. He fought at Trenton, Princeton, and Brandywine, winning Washington's commendation. At the Battle of Germantown he was intoxicated and was dismissed from the service.

"William Crawford was twenty-three when he served under Braddock. He was Washington's land agent and was with him on his 1770 trip to inspect his holdings in the Ohio Valley. He served as a colonel in the Revolution and took part in six major engagements.

"Colonel Crawford retired from the army but returned in 1782 to lead an expedition of 480 horsemen against the Sandusky, Ohio, rendezvous of the Indian allies of the British. His force panicked, and Colonel Crawford was captured. The Indians tied him to a pole by a long rope and tortured him for four hours before he died. He pleaded with the renegade Simon Girty to shoot him, but Girty refused.

"You now have sixteen names and four to go."

I turned up no additional names that week. When I suggested to my wife that she would enjoy spending a day or two researching in the Pennsylvania Room of the Library, she declined politely.

It was in this same conversation at the dinner table that a revealing incident happened. "Are you aware," I said, "that Presley Neville, the son of General John Neville, married Nancy Morgan, the daughter of General Daniel Morgan, his old comrade in arms?"

My wife replied, "That's nice, dear. We must invite them over some evening."

On the weekend, however, I was able to do my own research, and I turned up the seventeenth and eighteenth names.

Charles Lee was present at the battle as a twenty-four-year-old English officer. In few other battles in history were so many officers killed or wounded in proportion to the number engaged—sixty-two out of ninety-six—but Lee, like Washington, escaped unhurt.

Lee's career has been called "perhaps the strangest in the annals of the Revolution." His military experience won him a commission as the second of major generals; but he felt strongly that he deserved Washington's post as commander in chief. He repeatedly disregarded Washington's orders in several engagements, apparently in the hope of discrediting him. As a prisoner of war he traitorously helped British General William Howe draw up plans for taking Philadelphia—treachery which was not discovered until Howe's papers were published many years later. Exchanged, Lee continued in the American service until, because of disrespectful letters he wrote to General Washington and to Congress, he was court-martialed, suspended, and finally discharged.

Dr. Thomas Walker was commissary general to Braddock's Virginia troops and narrowly escaped losing his life in the battle. During the Revolution, Walker served on Virginia's Committee of Safety and Executive Council and was Albemarle County's representative in the House of Delegates. In Virginia his closest neighbor was Peter Jefferson; when Jefferson died in 1757, Walker became guardian of his fourteen-year-old son and for the next seven years watched over the growth and education of the young man who was to become the third President of the United States.

At this point, with only two names to go, I was forced to admit to Mr. G. that I was stalemated. To this he replied in a note.

"You have overlooked an important part of your material. General Braddock was defeated by a force of 72 French, 146 Canadians, and 637 Indians. Of these, only 30 were killed, mostly Indians, and some by falling tree branches cut off by stray English cannon balls.

"Now, consider this. The Ottawa Indians fought in the battle. Who was the great chief of the Ottawas? Pontiac. Pontiac was there.

"Pontiac had a notable diplomatic and military talent, but what was rare among Indians, a genius for organization. In 1763 he directed the largest and most powerful coalition in Indian history, and planned a simultaneous up-

rising against the twelve key forts on the frontier. All but a few of them fell, and for many months English power west of the mountains was limited to those at Detroit, Pittsburgh, and Ligonier."

I was disturbed by this and answered as follows:

"I don't think we can be *sure* that Pontiac was personally present at the Battle of the Monongahela. Parkman says in *Montcalm and Wolfe* that the chief 'possibly' commanded the Ottawas."

"Of course Pontiac was there," Mr. G. wrote back. "You don't think Ottawa Indians would fight without their leader, do you? And Pontiac was their leader, wasn't he? I'm willing to agree that we now have nineteen names. Let's get just one more little name, and we can rejoice and sleep undisturbed again."

I reviewed the careers of scores of men who could have been there, or should have been there, or who were there and never amounted to much afterwards. One by one, for various good reasons, I regretfully dismissed a half-dozen prime names. At last I said to my wife, "I know when I'm beaten. I am now going to forget the whole thing. I will begin to read the newspapers again. I will look at television. Nineteen names are enough."

"It really is too bad," she said, "after you worked so hard. Weren't there, by any chance, some famous survivors on the other side of the battle? I would think you could find at least one."

"We're counting the Indian chief," I said somewhat impatiently.

That was at dinner, and before dessert was served a possible solution struck me.

"I think I have it," I said. "The French!"

"Bully for you," said my wife.

I examined the records of the French officers known to be involved.

Captain Daniel Hyacinthe Marie Lienard de Beaujeu had just taken over command of Fort Duquesne from Captain Claude Pierre Pécaudy, sieur de Contrecoeur. Beaujeu, naked to the waist except for a piece of decorative armor at his neck, bounded over the hill, exchanged fire, deployed his men, and at the third volley was killed by a bullet through his head.

Contrecoeur, who had wanted to abandon Duquesne, remained within the fort during the entire engagement. On November 28, 1755, he was to write his minister of war from Montreal: "The Marquis de Vaudreuil doubtless has informed you, Monseigneur, of the last victory I gained on the 9th of last July at Fort Duquesne. . . . If my services seem of sufficient value to you, Monseigneur, to merit some reward, I dare ask you to bestow the Cross of St. Louis on me, and to further the promotion of my two children. . ." He did not become a famous man.

I turned to the biography of Dumas, the French officer who was second in command in the battle. I read with mounting interest, and then I wrote to Mr. G.:

"I now have the twentieth and final name of the illustrious persons who survived the Battle of July 9, 1755.

"It is Captain Jean-Daniel Dumas, who took command of the French forces when Captain Beaujeu fell. He brilliantly rallied his panicking Canadians and Indians, put them on the flanks of the enemy, and for some hours poured slaughtering fire into the helpless British ranks.

"Dumas became commandant of Fort Duquesne and, with Indian aid, vigorously harassed the English frontier.

"In 1759, the French king made Dumas a major general and inspector of all forces in Canada. After the fall of Montreal, Dumas returned to France, where he was promoted again. He became governor of Mauritius, the beautiful and strategically important island in the Indian Ocean, then owned by the French."

For the record, I put down the names of the twenty men who, by some remarkable conjunction of stars, met on the battlefield on the north bank of the Monongahela, survived, and went on to achieve personal distinction and a place in history. And I added:

"Of these twenty men, four had been at the Battle of Fort Necessity . . . eight were wounded at the Battle of the Monongahela . . . six were with General Forbes at the taking of Fort Duquesne . . . four fought at Quebec . . . six were intimately involved in Pontiac's Conspiracy . . . eight became general officers in the American Revolution . . . one became commander in chief of British forces . . . two were considered for the post of commander in chief of the Revolutionary forces . . . four made major historical contributions through their writings . . . one entered the U.S. Congress . . . and one became President of the United States."

About a week after this great moral victory I chanced to meet Mr. G. on his way to lunch. We walked down the street together.

"Life must be very dull for you," he said.

"For several days it was," I said, "but now I am deeply preoccupied with a strange and little-recognized circumstance of history which astonishes me every time I think of it."

"*Another* one?"

"I refer to the truly amazing number of prominent Americans, past and present, whose direct ancestors were survivors of the Battle of the Monongahela."

"Like for instance?"

"Well," I said, "like this. The builder of Blair House in Washington and the Postmaster General in Lincoln's Cabinet were both direct descendants of Christopher Gist. So was a man named States R. (for Rights) Gist, who played a prominent part in the secession movement and, as a brigadier general in the Confederate Army, was killed at the Battle of Franklin, Tennessee. And when a monument to General Braddock was put up and dedicated in 1913, one of the special honored guests at the ceremony was a gentleman named Monongahela de Beaujeu. I'd like to look into *him!*"

"Monongahela de Beaujeu," said Mr. G. in an awed voice.

"And, of course, there was B. Gratz Brown."

"B. Gratz *who?*"

"You mean you've never heard of B. Gratz Brown?" I said, concealing my triumph. "B. Gratz Brown, direct descendant of Christopher Gist, was only the Democratic vice presidential candidate on the Horace Greeley ticket, *that's* all B. Gratz Brown was."

Robert C. Alberts is a vice president of the advertising and public relations firm of Ketchum, MacLeod & Grove in Pittsburgh, Pennsylvania; a former editor of The Bulletin-Index Magazine, *a weekly news journal in Pittsburgh; and once a first lieutenant in the Army. His interlocutor, "Mr. G.," is George Ketchum, president of the firm. Neither of these gentlemen, to the best of our knowledge, is descended from any veteran of Braddock's Defeat.*

The Working Ladies of Lowell CONTINUED FROM PAGE 45

be considered that a few years in a mill was an honorable mode of securing a dower. The business could thus be conducted without any permanent manufacturing population. The operatives no longer form a separate caste, pursuing a sedentary employment, from parent to child, in the heated rooms of a factory; but are recruited, in a circulating current, from the healthy and virtuous population of the country.

In a circulating current! There was the trick. The fathers of Waltham had not invented the notion of an employer's personal responsibility for the physical and moral welfare of the worker. That was a legacy from indentured labor, apprenticeship—even slavery. But the new factory owners had built a new structure on that foundation. If they brought young girls to the factory for a brief period between maturing and marrying, and if they boarded them under safeguards approved by church, family, and all the gods of respectability, then a *rotating* labor force would escape the ills of industrial decay. It was simple country logic. Standing water stank; a running stream or a spring-fed pond stayed pure and clear.

So the experiment was tried at Waltham. Not much is known about early working conditions, but from a business viewpoint, success was enormous. The owners played a shrewd game from the start. They concentrated on plain and simple fabrics, marketed through a single firm, and they successfully lobbied, in 1816, for a certain measure of tariff protection. Francis Lowell died prematurely in 1817. He did not live to see another twenty years of dividends rarely falling below ten per cent, even while the price to the consumer dropped from twenty-one to six cents a yard. He did not need to; even by 1817, his kind of textile factory, mass-producing cheap, utilitarian goods, had won a clear decision over the dying system of decentralized craft production. By 1821, the leaders of the Boston Manufacturing Company were looking for new worlds to conquer, hunting for a site for a new factory, to turn out printed calicoes.

They found their spot in December of 1821, in a peaceable little farm community called East Chelmsford, some twenty-five miles from Boston. It was at the junction of the Concord and Merrimack rivers—a quiet place, where men could still fish tranquilly for salmon and alewives in their season. A no-longer-used canal around a fall in the Merrimack was quickly bought by the promoters of the new factory. It gave them water power and an iron grip on any future mill-building in the area. A new corporation, the Merrimack Manufacturing Company, was created—but its owners were predominantly the Waltham founders. For years they remained a well-knit group, holding tightly to patents and controlling blocks of stock, and admitting outsiders only when they could pass inspection—and pay!

But if the ownership elite did not grow swiftly, the enterprise did. The Merrimack factory was up in December of 1823. Within three years more, little East Chelmsford, with its scattered farmhouses, gristmills, store, and tavern, was ready for incorporation as a village. Its leading businessmen, landowners, and citizens—the mill owners, naturally—renamed it Lowell. And Lowell mushroomed, geysered, exploded. Two new mills went up in 1828, another in 1830, three more in 1831, still another in 1835. The population of 200 in 1820 jumped to 6,477 in 1830, and 17,633 in 1836. A bank appeared, then another, then a hotel, a library, two schoolhouses, and Episcopalian, Baptist, Congregational, Universalist, and Unitarian churches. In 1835 the Boston and Lowell Railroad—one of the country's earliest—was opened in a flourish of band music and spread-eagle oratory. By 1845 Lowell, population over 30,000, had become a modern factory town in less time than it took small boys who once had fished undisturbed in the Concord to reach the ripe age of thirty.

Lowell was more than a success. It was a showpiece. Its population consisted mostly of factory girls living in the company boardinghouses. From 1823 to about 1845, it seemed to show that the fond hopes of those who planned a rotating and virtuous labor force might be realized. Foreign tourists—Michel Chevalier of France, Harriet Martineau and Charles Dickens of England—and famous Americans like Andrew Jackson, Henry Clay, and David Crockett visited it to wonder and admire. The focus of attention was the band of New England country girls who had turned themselves into mill hands. They had done so for a number of reasons, among them to show, as one of their number put it, that "it is the laborer's privilege to ennoble his work by the aim with which he undertakes it, and by the enthusiasm and faithfulness he puts into it."

What kind of girls were they? Precisely as planned, they were farm girls, and not only did they come off the farms as expected, they went back to them according to prediction. In 1845 the author of a small book on Lowell inquired of several mill owners to learn whence came their "hands," and how long they stayed. In one factory employing 173 workers, 21 were from Massachusetts, 45 from Maine, 55 from New Hampshire, 52 from Vermont. Only five had worked more than ten years, and 114 of them—nearly two-thirds of the total force—had been there for less than four. Even allowing for some shifting from mill to mill, the turnover in Lowell's population was brisk.

The New England farmer's daughter was anything but a peasant. She might be classed technically as an "unskilled" laborer, but that was only so far as factory production was concerned. She could grow fruits and vegetables, and put them into pies and preserves of breathtaking quality. She could cook for one man or for twenty at harvest time. She could knit, sew, embroider, and sometimes spin and weave. She could keep a two-story frame house spotless, raise small animals and baby brothers and sisters, and nurse sick aunts and grannies as occasion demanded. She could make such varied household products as cheese, brooms, candles, and soap. Independence came as naturally to her as to her brothers, who at seventeen and eighteen were working their own fields or commanding fishing smacks, trading schooners, and whalers. She had the equivalent of a grade-school education, often kept her father's books if he was a small businessman on the side, and took as naturally as she breathed to reading

or to attending two-hour lectures and sermons.

One of these girls, Lucy Larcom, who later became a well-known poet and editor of a children's magazine, recalled her childhood in the port town of Newburyport. She remembered leisure hours spent in devouring Aesop, Bunyan, *Gulliver's Travels, The Vicar of Wakefield,* and *Arabian Nights.* The stories in them were no more wonderful than those that she got from retired seamen, who brought home gorgeously colored tropical parrots to squawk from perches in New England parlors, and who spoke to friends (addressed as "shipmate") about voyages to Calcutta and Hong Kong as casually as they might refer to a pony ride to the next village. Lucy knew the local farmers, too, who tramped into her father's store in thick boots and coarse trousers, smelling of hay, dung, and honest sweat. When her widowed mother moved to Lowell to run one of the boardinghouses, Lucy, aged eleven, was prepared for hard work and for leisure rigorously spent in self-improvement.

In the mills there was work in plenty. From April to October, operations began about 5 A.M. and ran until close to 7:30 in the evening, with half-hour interruptions for breakfast at 7 A.M. and dinner at 12:30 in the afternoon. In the shorter months, breakfast was served before daylight, and the working day was finished under lamps. Six days of eleven to thirteen hours' actual work made a long week, but not necessarily a prohibitive one to girls used to being up with the rooster and rarely idle until the sewing basket was set aside for nine o'clock bedtime. (The American factory schedule, in fact, copied farmer's hours—up at dawn to feed stock before breakfast, home for dinner in hottest daytime, late supper after barnyard chores.)

Nor was the factory work unremittingly taxing. Lucy's first job was as a bobbin girl, watching a spinning frame and replacing filled spools with empty ones. It was almost fun to watch a bobbin wax fat, and lift it off at the right moment. Those at spooling, warping, and dressing machines had harder work. The "buzzing and hissing and whizzing of pulleys and rollers and spindles and flyers . . . often grew tiresome." But a lucky girl, near a window, could tend flowers in a window box or read (when such things were permitted, as they were at first) or simply daydream. Daydreaming was discouraged, of course, for one real purpose of having attendants at the machinery was to watch for broken threads, overfilled bobbins, twisted belts, spindles that slipped off their shafts—any one of which could in seconds create an ungodly jam of twisted fibers and stalled machinery.

At the looms, the girls had more to watch—warp threads rising and falling regularly to the tug of the heddles, shuttles jerking back and forth between the warp threads at an even 120 picks to the minute, warp-beam and cloth-beam rolling, and reed beating the cross-threads tight together in even thumps. A wary eye was needed here for breaks and snarls, and for shuttle boxes that needed to be changed; but if a girl had only one or two looms to tend, it was not overly burdensome. Then there were other jobs of varying skill and distastefulness—from minding the whippers and pickers which fluffed the newly arrived cotton, to folding, measuring, and packing finished goods in the cloth room. When Lucy Larcom grew up, she chose to work there. It paid less than machine-tending, but left more quiet hours for reading; an overseer once found his intellectual little mill girl deeply absorbed in Cotton Mather's pedantic *Magnalia Christi Americana* while she was folding cloth.

For the girl who grew a little weary of it all, it was always possible to go home for a month or two. With Lowell booming and growing, there would always be a job when she returned to the factory. What was more, farm girls did not need to accept assignments that they regarded as unfair. A young woman who knew that she was only a day's trip from home, where there were chickens in the henyard, milk in the springhouse, and squash in the garden, took no "sass" from an overseer. Early mill records duly chronicled the dismissal of some girls for "insolence," which undoubtedly meant telling overseers what they thought of them. Wherever industry had not completely displaced a rural way of life, workers had an extra bit of protection. The English-woman, Harriet Martineau, noted that the boot and shoe makers of Lynn, Massachusetts, as late as 1835, knocked off in summers to earn money by fishing. In Pennsylvania in the 1820's, the overseer at an iron foundry carefully recorded that a batch of molten iron had been ruined because, when it was ready to pour, nobody was on hand. "The men," he sorrowfully noted, "was out hunting with their guns."

And if, somehow, the hours did seem to stretch a bit toward the close of the day, there were the tangible rewards in cash to consider. It is not easy to generalize about Lowell wages from 1830 to 1845, particularly since much of the pay was by the piece. In 1840 a careful Scot, James Montgomery, made a study of the comparative costs of cotton manufacture in Great Britain and the United States. He estimated that American owners had to figure on paying girls at various spinning machines $2.50 to $3.50 a week. Weavers could earn twenty-five cents per "piece," which meant that a girl who was willing to work an extra loom might earn as much as $4.50 or even $5.50. (The gap in pay between the rank and file and the "non-coms" in the industrial army was not very great. Bookkeepers rated

$9.50 weekly, overseers $12, and superintendents $25. It seems safe to say that the mill girls, in this period, averaged $3.50 a week in wages. In Lowell in 1840, five cents bought a half-dozen eggs, fifteen cents an entire chicken, and two dollars a carcass of mutton. The companies charged the girls $1.25 for their board and lodging, which left $2.25—nearly $5 every fortnight, or $9 every month, according to how paydays fell—for spending or for saving.

In rural New England a century and a quarter ago, that was no inconsiderable sum of cash. The girls saved what must have been a considerable amount of it. In 1845, according to the Reverend Henry Miles in his *Lowell As It Was And As It Is,* half of the two thousand depositors in the Lowell Savings Bank were factory girls, and their bankbooks showed a total of more than $100,000 laid away. Between 1829 and 1845, the bank had taken in $2,103,-500 and paid out $1,423,500, much of it in the girls' earnings. The girls used this money for their own dowries; they lifted mortgages from fathers' farms; they supported fatherless nephews, nieces, and cousins; and, apparently not infrequently, they put brothers through college.

Francis Cabot Lowell

But what counted was not whether the girls spent their pay on ribbons and shawls or saved it for the future. What counted was that as women, they had money of their own. This was an age when a woman's property was still in the absolute control of her husband, and when the single or widowed woman who did not choose to become a seamstress or a housemaid lived on family charity. Another of those literate mill girls, Harriet Hanson Robinson, summed up the advantages of having one's own income:

The law took no cognizance of woman as a money-spender. She was a ward, an appendage, a relict. Thus it happened, that if a woman did not choose to marry, or, when left a widow, to re-marry, she had no choice but to enter one of the few employments open to her, or to become a burden on the charity of some relative. . . . The cotton-factory was a great opening to these lonely and dependent women. . . . At last they had found a place in the universe; they were no longer obliged to finish out their faded lives mere burdens to male relatives. . . . For the first time in this country woman's labor had a money value. . . . And thus a long upward step in our material civilization was taken; woman had begun to earn and hold her own money, and through its aid had learned to think and to act for herself.

Harriet remembered what a blessing the factory was to those unhappy and lonely older women who sat in New England chimney corners, meekly enduring the teasing of the children, the gruffness of the men, and the sharpness of female in-laws who had kitchens and hearthsides of their own. Some went into the factories, and

. . . after the first pay-day came, and they felt the jingle of silver in their pockets, and had begun to feel its mercurial influence, their bowed heads were lifted, their necks seemed braced with steel, they looked you in the face, sang blithely among their looms or frames, and walked with elastic step to and from work.

To talk of wage slavery to such women was futile; to them the factory gates had opened the way to independence.

When work was done, the girls returned to the boardinghouses. They were usually two or three story frame buildings, standing in neat rows separated from the factory by squares of greenery. They were run by older women, often widows like Mrs. Larcom, or like the mothers of Nathaniel Banks and Benjamin F. Butler, both of whom were to become Massachusetts political leaders and Civil War generals. The houses had kitchens attached in the back, dining rooms and parlors on the ground floor, and bedrooms in which two or four girls roomed together.

They did not seem to regard that a hardship. Companionship, as a matter of fact, took the sting out of initial homesickness. Harriet Robinson remembered how the wagons which had gone into the back country to recruit would pull up before a boardinghouse and discharge a cluster of farm girls, followed by a pile of neat, small trunks, often bound in home-tanned, spotted calfskin on which the hair still showed. The new arrivals would gaze wide-eyed and white-faced at the huge buildings, the crowds, and the rushing canal. As an old woman, Harriet still recalled one girl with a large tear in each eye, pathetically clutching a bandbox on which the name "Plumy Clay" was carefully lettered.

Yet after a few weeks in which Plumy and Samantha and Keziah and Elgardy and Leafy and Ruhamah had come to be friends, it all seemed rather adventuresome. The girls chatted in their rooms in the evening, or sometimes read to each other from books that might have been found on the shelves of any middle-class home of the period. There were such "holy" works as Baxter's *Saints' Rest,* and *Pilgrim's Progress,* of course, but in addition, such popular (and less uplifting) novels as *Charlotte Temple, The Castle of Otranto,* and *The Mysteries of Udolpho.* On the table in the parlor were the newspapers to which the girls jointly sub-

scribed—religious sheets like the *Christian Register, Christian Herald,* and *Signs of the Times,* abolitionist journals such as *The Liberator* and *Herald of Freedom,* and ordinary dailies like the *Boston Daily Times.* The mill girls read and discussed the contents of these organs of opinion, and debated among themselves the fads and fancies of the yeasty 1830's and 1840's—phrenology, mesmerism, Grahamism, Fourierism. One boardinghouse even contained a Mormon Bible!

Undoubtedly it was only a small number of the girls who were grimly intellectual, but they gave a tone to the entire enterprise. They were the ones who went to lectures at the lyceum in Lowell, and solemnly took note of the pearls of wisdom that fell from the lips of John Quincy Adams, Edward Everett, Ralph Waldo Emerson, John Greenleaf Whittier, and the other gods of New England. They were the girls who took books into the factories, and later, when this was tabooed, pasted pages of newspaper poetry to their looms and frames and memorized as they worked. Some girls felt that the Bible ought to be exempt from the rule, and brought their pocket Testaments to work, creating a nice problem for pious overseers. Under the rules, they had to confiscate all literature discovered, but it went hard for some to wrest the Scriptures from a girl. "I did think," said one of them ruefully to a victim of such a seizure, "you had more conscience than to bring that book in here." One group of these "factory ladies," relentlessly bent upon improving each shining hour, flabbergasted Charles Dickens (who visited Lowell in 1841) by clubbing together to buy a piano for their boardinghouse parlor. The novelist was not merely confounded by such a genteel instrument in what was, after all, a home for "working-class" women, but he shared the amazement which a modern reader must feel that girls who worked a fourteen-hour day could be interested in anything more taxing in the evening than climbing wearily into bed.

Perhaps the most astonishing fact of all was that some of the girls, after a dawn-to-dusk session in the mill, not only found time to read literature, but to make it. Some of the ministers whose congregations included a sprinkling of highly literate mill girls had taken the lead in forming "improvement circles" as early as 1838. At the meetings of these groups—as in the literary clubs of the colleges of that day—members read their own compositions to each other for mutual criticism. The Reverend Abel Thomas, of Lowell's First Universalist Church, gradually accumulated a drawerful of essays, short stories, and poems by the members of his "circle." Enthused by what he read, he raised enough money to issue a collection of the pieces in a pamphlet entitled *The Lowell Offering.* Some of the money came from the company, which sensed the publicity value of the scheme, in the form of a large order for copies.

Having still more material on hand, Thomas undertook to edit the *Offering* as a regular periodical. Four numbers appeared in 1840 and 1841. Meanwhile an "improvement circle" in the First Congregationalist Church had independently launched an *Operatives' Magazine*. In 1842, the Reverend Mr. Thomas turned the editorship of the *Offering* over completely to two of the millworkers, Harriot F. Curtis and Harriet Farley. Presumably, he wanted to prove once and for all that the "operatives" could write, edit, and publish a magazine entirely under their own power. The two women merged the *Lowell Offering* and *Operatives' Magazine,* and managed to run it for five volumes. It finally died, as conditions began to change in Lowell, and a few efforts to revive it under other titles failed.

The *Lowell Offering* was by no means the cream of American periodical literature of the mid-nineteenth century. Yet it was an incredible production to emerge from a factory working force. It contained, Harriet Robinson recalled, "allegories, poems, conversations on physiology, astronomy, and other scientific subjects, dissertations on poetry, and on the beauties of nature, didactic pieces on highly moral and religious subjects, translations from French and Latin, stories of factory and other life, sketches of local New England history, and sometimes chapters of a novel." The poetry was in the mold of popular female bards of the period like Lydia Sigourney; the prose had overtones of Addison, Goldsmith, and the briskly selling lady novelist, Lydia Maria Child. The fifty-seven girls who contributed to it chose pen names as far from "Harriet," "Lucy," "Abby," and "Sarah" as they could get—"Ella," "Adelaide," "Aramantha," "Oriana," "Dolly Dindle," and "Grace Gayfeather." Two or three of the contributors

continued as writers in later life; others became missionaries, schoolteachers, and suffragettes, and at least one—Margaret Foley—was a successful sculptor.

All of this was a long way from the factory slums of Birmingham and Manchester, which, in those very 1840's, were furnishing ammunition for the assaults on capitalism of Engels and Marx. The girls were aware of their uniqueness, and in the brief moments between sleep and work they undertook their mental cultivation proudly and self-consciously. They were, in their own eyes, pioneers, demonstrating that "woman" could be independent, that "manual labor" could be combined with character and intellect, and that the "impossible" concept of a highly educated working class was realizable in the United States. *They* knew that in their dignity and pride they were the equals of the capitalists who employed them, whatever their incomes. Their writing and poetizing and piano playing were meant to prove, as Lucy Larcom said, that "honest work has no need to assert itself or to humble itself in a nation like ours, but simply to take its place as one of the foundation-stones of the republic." At Brook Farm, not too far from Lowell, a number of better-educated men and women were conducting an experiment that was not too different. Pitching hay in the afternoons and reading Greek in the evenings in West Roxbury were ways of vindicating the dignity of labor, too. (*See* "A Season in Utopia," AMERICAN HERITAGE, April, 1959.)

And so, willingly, the girls accepted the discipline of the boardinghouses. They went to church regularly, were in by 10 P.M., avoided improper conduct and language, and shunned idle companions—all of which came to them easily enough. They were trying to make of their factory community "a rather select industrial school for young people," Lucy Larcom wrote in 1889. And then she added, proudly: "The girls were just such

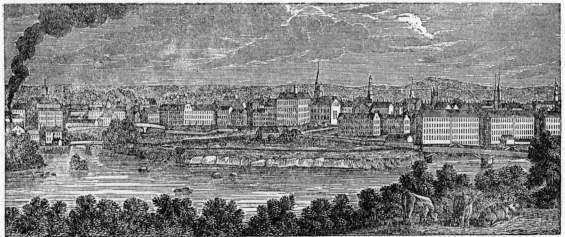

The mills of Lowell crowded the banks of the Merrimack in 1839.

girls as are knocking at the doors of young women's colleges today."

So there was Lowell in 1845 at its high noon, and whether the credit belonged to the tariff or American democracy or creative capital or the frontier or Jehovah who smiled upon America was hard to say. It was not really typical of the growing factory system. But all observers agreed that it was a sight to admire. President Jackson visited Lowell in June of 1833, and rode under triumphal arches amid a procession of drums, militiamen, citizens, schoolchildren, and 2,500 of the factory girls, carrying parasols and wearing stockings of silk. Reputedly Jackson swore that "by the Eternal," they were pretty women. Congressman Crockett of Tennessee came the next year, and if we can believe the statement in the largely fraudulent *Autobiography* ghostwritten for him, found the girls "well-dressed, lively, and genteel," looking as if "they were coming from a quilting frolic." Henry Clay came to beam at the success, in 1834, of the domestic manufactures whose protection he had so long and eloquently advocated.

Charles Dickens, as late as 1841, found that the whole city still had a fresh, new appearance (except for the mud). Its shiny buildings looked like those of a cardboard toy town, fresh out of the wrappings. He inspected the factories, he watched the girls at work, and he carried off four hundred pages of the *Offering* to read. Dickens disliked industrialism, and at that time he disliked the United States. He would have been glad, undoubtedly, to pour a little humanitarian spite on an exploitative American industrialism. But after looking long and hard, he declared: "I cannot recall or separate one young face that gave me a painful impression; not one young girl whom, assuming it to be a matter of necessity that she should gain her daily bread by the labour of her hands, I would have removed from those works if I had had the power."

In another twenty years Dickens' thoughts might have been different. For shortly after that first visit of his, Lowell began to decline. The cotton factories moved away from the golden day, toward the era of Lawrence, the Pemberton Mill disasters, and bitterness.

The change came gradually, but even in the heyday a sharp eye might have seen the warning signals going up. There was, to begin with, an iron streak in the companies' paternalism. Their control of the force was as rigid as that of any army. Girls who quit "properly," giving their employer two weeks' notice, received an "honorable discharge" (the very words entered on company records) signed by their superintendent. Not a single mill would hire an experienced worker without such a discharge, which meant that a girl who was

CULVER PICTURES

Cotton-weaving looms had been improved by 1857, when this engraving appeared in The Family Christian Almanac, *but the lives of the mill girls had become harder. Few had time —or permission—to tend flower pots on the window sills.*

fired, or left for any reason not approved by her employers, was barred from factory work for good. It also meant that there was no competitive bidding among bosses, and no way of improving conditions, therefore, except as the bosses chose. And since the companies did not hesitate to discharge girls who received bad conduct reports from the boardinghouse matrons, their "stewardship" sometimes became a kind of punitive spying into the employees' personal lives.

As the bloom wore off the noble experiment, there were murmurs of discontent. Fourteen hours of daily indoor work, broken only for two hastily gulped meals, took some of the spring out of the millworkers. Those whose health broke down could enter a company-built hospital, but had to pay three dollars a week for the privilege, and often emerged with a heavy debt to be worked off. The hardy few who had energy left to enjoy the "advantages" of the boardinghouses began to leave. Labor reformer Seth Luther sardonically compared those who remained to the horse of a hardfisted farmer, who explained that his animal had "a bushel and a half of oats, *only he ain't got no time to eat 'em.*" Luther, and others like him, resented the corporation owners' growing sense of superiority, however patriarchal it might be. A small but articulate labor press denounced the "mushroom aristocracy of New England, who so arrogantly aspire to lord it over God's heritage."

The real sin of the mushroom aristocrats, however, was nothing so impalpable as an attitude. The truth was that as early as 1836, in the face of growing competition, they began to cut costs at the expense of the workers. In that year the wages of the Lowell mill girls were reduced by a dollar each week. Some 1,500 girls staged a "turn-out" in protest. It was a decorous enough affair: they walked through the streets waving their handkerchiefs and singing a parody of a popular tune:

Oh! isn't it a pity, such a pretty girl as I—
Should be sent to the factory to pine away and die?
Oh! I cannot be a slave,
I will not be a slave,
For I'm so fond of liberty
That I cannot be a slave.

It was charming, intelligent, and utterly futile. The companies did not restore the cuts—then or later. In addition, they began to increase the number of frames and looms each girl had to watch, and then to overcrowd the boardinghouses, assigning as many as eight to a room. The operatives began, after all, to look like the washed-out and exhausted creatures of Jefferson's most dire predictions.

For the girls who had come on the scene early, of course, there was the option of going home. That appealed to them even more than striking, which had an unladylike and un-Christian character about it, hardly becoming to the virtuous daughters of independent yeomen. They would return to the farm until the owners, short of hands, saw reason. In time, the girls believed, they must see it, for in America there was no "irrepressible conflict" between capital and labor.

So the more aggressive and independent girls drifted away from Lowell. But the owners were not concerned with the problem of replacements. For in the 1840's a mighty tide of immigration was setting in, much of it Irish. A few of Erin's sons had been in Lowell in Lucy Larcom's day—some six hundred in 1835—living with their large families in shanties on the town's fringe. Sometimes on their way to work Lucy and her friends would toss a slice of boardinghouse bread to an elderly Irishwoman in order to elicit a musical flood of grateful brogue.

There was nothing quaint about the effect of the Irish on the labor market, however. By 1860 they constituted nearly half the population of Lowell. There were no friendly farms to which *they* could retreat when conditions worsened. The roofs that they could call their own were in Lowell only, and they were not the decent roofs of the boardinghouses, but overcrowded, jerry-built, or decaying homes. The companies were spared the expense of boardinghouses in this way, a point not lost upon them. And the millowners did not worry especially about the "moral character" of their Hibernian operatives, being quite willing to leave that to the priests and the police.

While the labor force thus changed, so did the nature of the owning group. The new ownership was well represented by a man like Amos Lawrence, ancestor of many pious churchmen, whose name was bestowed on a new mill town on the Merrimack, built up in the 1840's. Lawrence was a nonsmoker and nondrinker who demanded the same abstinence of his male employees. Plagued with stomach trouble, he dined briefly and frugally on watery gruel, and he was not a man to listen sympathetically to complaints that a worker's salary did not buy an adequate diet. Reproached by some critics with his great wealth, he is said to have snarled: "There is one thing you may as well understand; I know how to make money, and *you* cannot prevent it." There was something hard here that made the older, paternalistic, nationalistic outlook of the founders of Waltham seem archaic. The difference between Lawrence and Lowell, the towns, was something like the difference between Lawrence and Lowell, the men.

In addition, as stockholding in the corporations finally became a little more widespread, the personal link between owner and worker was snapped. The original Boston promoters had been drawn from the same Yankee stock as the mill hands. But the difference between a Boston attorney with a few shares of Suffolk Manufacturing Company in his safe, and Bridget Doyle at her spinning frame, was more than one of money. It was a gap between ways of life and understanding. Moreover, as some stock passed into the hands of guardians and estate administrators, company treasurers were at last able to invoke piously the interests of widows and orphans, as they maintained dividends while slashing wages and stretching out tasks.

Through the 1850's the labor scene darkened as industry spread through the nation. Prices rose in response to gold strikes and industrial booms, but wages remained at ancient levels. Factory workers struck more frequently—and were more frequently replaced by immigrant strikebreakers. Some leaders, despairing of direct action by labor, turned to state legislatures and petitioned for laws restricting the hours of labor and the employment of women and children. Some small gains were made in legislative cutting of the work burden of children under twelve, but most "ten-hour" legislation proposed in New England in the fifties died in the state capitals. The slogans of progress which had justified the beginnings of Waltham and Lowell now rang out to justify a *status quo* maintained at the price of increasing bitterness.

So it was that in 1860 something more than a single

defectively built factory lay in ruins in Lawrence. In all New England there was evidence that the United States was going to have to find another way toward justice for labor—was going to have to walk the long road through decades of violence, organization, degradation, cruelty, bitterness, and protest, before the light would dawn again. The short cut to Utopia had run into a dead end, and Lowell was not, as it turned out, the harbinger of a perfect, harmonious, and just industrial society, in which a "circulating current" of laborers gained bread, education, and stature at the machines. It was not the only utopian experiment of the Jacksonian era to fail. Like the others, it remains in American history as a memory, the surviving token of a lost innocence that believed in the impossible, and for a few short hours in a simpler time, seemed to make it work.

Bernard A. Weisberger, associate professor of history at the University of Chicago, is the author of Reporters for the Union *and* They Gathered at the River. *He is completing a new book,* The American Newspaperman, *to be published in the Chicago History of American Civilization Series.*

For further reading: The Lowells and Their Seven Worlds, *by Ferris Greenslet (Houghton Mifflin, 1949);* Golden Threads, *by Hannah Josephson (Duell, Sloan and Pearce, 1949);* The Early New England Cotton Manufacture, *by Caroline Ware (Houghton Mifflin, 1931).*

The Storming of the Alamo CONTINUED FROM PAGE 33

corn to eat—no coffee, sugar, or salt. The remnant of the council, adjourning in mid-February, denounced them as "insurgents to the government"; it had never sent them supplies of any kind.

Why, then, did they remain at their post?

There is an answer, given a little earlier in a sort of manifesto signed by a few of them:

We, the undersigned, have embarked on board the schooner Santiago, on December 9, 1835, at New Orleans, for Texas, to relieve our oppressed brethren who have emigrated thither by inducements held forth to them by the Mexican government, and rights guaranteed to settlers of that province, which that government now denies them; and in our opinion, their situation is assimilated to that of our fathers, who labored under tyrannical oppression. Resolved, that we have left every endearment, as our respective places of abode in the United States of America, to maintain and defend our brethren, at the peril of our lives, liberties and fortunes. . . . We declare these as our sentiments and determination.

Seldom in time of war has a garrison so tiny been so isolated.

To the north, as far as the Arctic ice, was Indian country. To the east the sparsely settled American colonies began at Gonzales, seventy miles away, with no habitation in between. To the southeast, one hundred miles away, near the Gulf of Mexico, the stalled Matamoros expedition waited for supplies that never came. Two-thirds of its members joined with groups just arrived from the United States, gathering, through February, at Goliad (an old Spanish fort) under the command of James Fannin, until their number passed 400. The remainder hunted wild horses at San Patricio, an abandoned Irish colony fifty miles south of Goliad.

To the west and southwest of the Alamo stretched 150 miles of mesquite, prickly pear, rattlesnakes, and Indians. Then, along the Rio Grande, a few Mexican towns were scattered. South of the river, beyond deserts and rugged *sierras,* larger towns were widely separated, and in several of these Santa Anna was assembling, feverishly and not always by gentle persuasion, men, money, and supplies. Early in February he had more than 7,000 troops at points, including Matamoros on the coast, from which he could hurl them against Texas.

His darkening shadow in the west was not unperceived by any of the three officers who, in succession, had some charge of the tiny garrison at the Alamo. They were kept informed by certain friendly Mexican citizens of San Antonio who traded across the Rio Grande. In his first reports, early in January, Colonel Neill warned the governor of enemy troop concentrations. Bowie's warning was more ominous. Travis, in his report of February 12, pointed out accurately the size and progress of the threatening forces.

It has been said that the officers in the Alamo "allowed themselves to be surprised" by Santa Anna. But even with a much larger garrison and many more horses, it would have been impossible to guard all the trails from the Rio Grande.

They could not have known that Santa Anna would drive his troops through a snowstorm and searing heat, across deserts, without adequate rations and without any medicines, the sick being heaped on pack animals, dead men and mules left strewn along the way. They could not have known, yet, the full measure of his contempt for human life, except his own.

Relations had been friendly between the San Antonio Mexicans and the men of the Alamo. They attended fandangos and cockfights together. Travis, proud of his Spanish, wrote: "The citizens have every confidence in me, because they can communicate with me, & have shown every disposition to aid me with all they have." Some joined the Texas Army, and three more were to die in the Alamo. But the approach of Santa Anna's army brought with it a chill.

San Antonio was a town of some two thousand Spanish-speaking people, mainly herdsmen and horsemen, who loved dancing, gambling, racing, and religious festivals. They remembered the cruelties of a Spanish army (Santa Anna was with it as a young lieutenant) that had sacked the town in 1813. They did not wish to see a repetition.

By the middle of February, Bowie, as commander of the volunteers, and Travis, as commander of the Regulars and the cavalry, were signing a joint appeal for money, provisions, men.

On the evening of February 21, Santa Anna and the advance guard of his army reached the bank of the Medina River, some twenty miles southwest of San Antonio. Heavy rains kept him from crossing for two days. Then, about noon on February 23, a sentinel posted in the tower of the parish church on Main Plaza sounded the bell. He said he had seen a "glittering, as of lances" in the west. Two horsemen rode out and reported a company of Mexican cavalry in formation, "their polished armor glistening in the rays of the sun," an officer riding up and down in front of them waving his sword, as if giving orders.

About two o'clock in the afternoon Santa Anna's advance guard entered the town. Bowie, Travis, and their men were in the Alamo. With them were several friendly Mexicans, including women and children; also the wife and infant daughter of Almeron Dickinson, captain of artillery. On their way in, the men had rounded up a herd of beeves and found some corn stored in the houses. Within the enclosure they had opened up a well. They would not lack for food of a sort, nor water. There was a scene of wild confusion, with men clamoring for arms and no semblance of order; the swearing was phenomenal.

About three o'clock a blood-red flag, meaning NO QUARTER, was hoisted on the tower of the parish church. Travis replied from the Alamo with a cannon shot. The next day, February 24, he sent out his famous message "to the People of Texas and all the Americans in the World":

Fellow citizens & compatriots, I am besieged by a thousand or more of the Mexicans under Santa Anna—I have sustained a continual Bombardment & cannonade for 24 hours & have not lost a man—The enemy has demanded a Surrender at discretion, otherwise the garrison are to be put to the sword, if the fort is taken. . . . *I shall never surrender or retreat.*

Among the flags flying at the Alamo during the final siege was that of the New Orleans Grays.

Then, I call on you in the name of Liberty, of patriotism & everything dear to the American character to come to our aid, with all dispatch—The enemy is receiving reinforcements daily & will no doubt increase to three or four thousand in four or five days.

If this call is neglected, I am determined to sustain myself as long as possible & die like a soldier who never forgets what is due to his own honor or that of his country—
Victory or Death.

He meant every word of it.

A cold wind blew from the north on the night of February 25, chilling the blanketless men in the Alamo. Bowie, who had been hurt by a cannon ball that had rolled from a platform, was put to bed with pneumonia. Travis now had sole command.

On the twenty-fifth the enemy attempted to set up a battery in front of the Alamo's south gate. The defenders made a sally and killed some soldiers. After dark the enemy charged the north wall and were repulsed with musket shot and grape. A detachment of cavalry attempting to cross the river on a narrow bridge was blasted by the Alamo guns and a Mexican colonel, knocked into the water, nearly drowned.

During the first four days of the siege the defenders made sallies, burned huts near the walls, and fought the attackers hand to hand when necessary. But after February 26 they were hedged in by artillery; the bombardment let up at intervals, only to resume with increased fury.

Davy Crockett entertained the men with his fiddle; but he did not like to be penned up. "I think we had better march out of here and die in the open air," he would say.

But if the main body of defenders was pinned down, couriers could still go in and out. Travis sent a rider to Goliad, but there Fannin was in no position to help anyone; on February 27 and March 2 the remnants of the Matamoros expedition were killed or captured at and near San Patricio. Travis also appealed to the colonists at Gonzales, and he had some success. On March 1 a band of thirty-two volunteers, some of them boys, somehow found their way into the Alamo.

On March 3 Travis wrote his last letters and sent them out by couriers. He said the garrison had been "miraculously preserved"; he had not lost a man. But two 9-pounders near the town were tearing holes in the walls with every shot. He heard sounds of rejoicing in the town, where 2,000 reinforcements for Santa Anna had just arrived. When he heard the bell of the parish church ringing, he did not know it was for the annihilation of the Americans at San Patricio, but in any case he had given up hope of aid from Fannin: "I look to the colonies alone for aid; unless it arrives soon I shall have to fight the enemy on his terms. I feel confident that the determined valor and desperate courage of my men will not fail them in the last struggle; and although they may be sacrificed to the vengeance of a Gothic enemy, the victory will cost the enemy so dear, it will be worse for him than a defeat."

That same day, March 3, Travis is said to have drawn a line with his sword on the ground, and to have asked those who would stay in the Alamo to the end, even though the cause was hopeless, to step over the line and stand beside him. The story has been told separately by three alleged eyewitnesses, but historians have scorned it as "theatrical" and "improbable." Whatever the truth of it, the story goes on to relate that just one man stepped back, and later made his escape. Bowie asked his companions to carry his cot across the line so he could be with them.

On the same day, Santa Anna had heavy guns placed within musket range of the Alamo's north wall; despite the popular assumption that nobody was hurt in eleven days of shelling, skeletons in buckskin tatters dug up from the floor of the church years afterward should be proof that the Mexican artillery was effective. "Men died there, and women," said Enrique Esparza, the twelve-year-old son of one of the Alamo's gunners. "Even children died there."

In the dark of night the Mexican troops would feign assaults. Sudden yells, cheers, and fusillades would keep the defenders off balance. Then, on the night of March 5, a roaring cannonade shook the Alamo, followed by a long spell of stillness to lull senses aching for sleep. At five the next morning, in the dark and the cold, a bugle shrilled from the north and suddenly, from four sides, came the tramping of massed feet, thousands of feet, advancing at a run.

The assault was intended to be a surprise, but raw recruits yelled "*Viva* Santa Anna!" and the cannon of the Alamo blazed. One Mexican soldier saw forty of his comrades fall around him. The mass surged against the walls and broke, screaming. From the rear, fusiliers who aimed too low shot their own storm troops in the back of the head. They toppled from the ladders. A wounded Mexican colonel, urging his men on, was trampled to death.

Again the columns were driven forward. The alcalde of San Antonio, whom Santa Anna had ordered to wait behind the Mexican lines to look after the dead and wounded, saw the second assault shattered by the "deadly fire of Travis' artillery, which resembled a constant thunder."

The slaughter had gone on for nearly two hours when Santa Anna gave word to pull back his haggled ranks. He called up his reserves.

"At the third charge," said the alcalde, "the battalion of Toluca began to scale the walls and suffered severely: Out of 800 men only 130 were left alive." Then, according to the account written later by General Filisola, the columns attacking the east and west sides joined the force on the north "by a spontaneous movement," smashed over the cannon, and poured through the breach.

Travis fell on the gun there, "a single bullet wound in his forehead."

When the defenders turned "a small cannon on a high platform" to stem the breakthrough on the north, the Mexican column on the south side, "taking clever advantage of the protection offered by some little houses of mud and stone near the southwest angle, by a daring move seized the cannon [the 18-pounder] embrasured in that angle, and through the port entered the plaza." Other troops "poured over the walls like sheep."

Santa Anna now approached close enough to observe that "the brisk fire of musketry illuminated the interior of the fortress, its walls and ditches."

The men in the Alamo abandoned their artillery, useless now at such short range. In the vast, bare plaza, the size of a city block, they were few and scattered and utterly exposed. There was no chance to reload their rifles or muskets. So they clubbed their assailants with the stocks as they ran for the two-story stone building on the east side of the plaza.

Here preparation had been made for a final stand. Within each of the five arched doors opening west in the "long barracks" was a semicircular parapet of stakes shoring a double curtain of rawhide rammed with earth. The Mexican troops, said Filisola, turned the captured guns against this building, "in which the rebels had taken refuge, and from which they were firing on the troops that were climbing down into the plaza. And within these doors, by grapeshot, musket-shot and the bayonet, they were all killed at last."

But not quite all, yet. The church in the southeast corner of the enclosure held a few defenders. There lay the stricken Bowie. The women and children were there: Mexicans of San Antonio except for Mrs. Dickinson, holding her child in her arms. She knelt and prayed, clutching the child, in the narrow, vaulted sacristy, now filled with smoke. Pursued by Mexican troops, two boys, eleven and twelve years old, ran into the room with their father, a gunner. The father begged for mercy, but the soldiers ran him through and carried the boys out of the room on their bloody bayonets. Another gunner ran in; they shot him "and four Mexican soldiers stuck their bayonets into his body and raised him up into the air like a farmer does a bundle of fodder when he loads it into a wagon."

In the small adjoining room, Bowie, from his cot, fired until his body, too, was riddled with bullets.

The father of twelve-year-old Enrique Esparza had been killed beside his cannon, which had been embrasured in the window of the south transept of the church. There was hand-to-hand fighting in the dark, the Mexicans rushing the defenders with bayonets. "It was pitch dark there," said young Esparza. "After the soldiers of Santa Anna had got all the women and children huddled in the southwest corner of the church, they stood still and fired into the darkness. They kept on firing at the men who had defended the Alamo. For fully a quarter of an hour, and until someone brought lanterns, they kept on firing on them, after all the defenders had been slain, and their corpses were lying still."

The Mexican women were taken to Santa Anna, questioned, and released. Mrs. Dickinson and her child were treated kindly.

Five "foreigners," found hiding, were brought before Santa Anna; he upbraided the officer who had spared them, then turned his back. Soldiers set on them with bayonets.

"After all the dead Mexicans were taken out of the Alamo," said the alcalde, "Santa Anna ordered wood to be brought to burn the bodies of the Texans. He sent a company of dragoons with me to bring wood and dry branches from the neighboring forest. About 3 o'clock in the afternoon they commenced laying the wood and dry branches, upon which a file of dead bodies was placed. More wood was piled on them and another file brought, and in this manner they were arranged in layers. Kindling wood was distributed throughout the pile, and about 5 o'clock in the evening it was lighted.

"The dead Mexicans of Santa Anna were taken to the graveyard, but not having sufficient room for them, I ordered some of them to be thrown into the river,

The Mexican flag carried by Santa Anna featured a golden eagle from Aztec mythology.

which was done on the same day. Santa Anna's loss was estimated at 1,600. These were the flower of his army." (This estimate is too high, even counting both dead and wounded.)

"The men burned numbered 182. I was an eyewitness, for as alcalde of San Antonio, I was with some of the neighbors collecting the dead bodies and placing them on the funeral pile."

Travis had said, three days before he died, "Victory will cost the enemy so dear, it will be worse for him than a defeat." Santa Anna's frightful losses did not deter him from driving his army on through Texas. But the slaughter of the men in the Alamo shocked the colonists out of their apathy.

On March 13 scouts from Gonzales met Mrs. Dickinson on the prairie. She had been given a horse and sent with an intimidating message for the colonists. That night the frontier town was a choir of grief.

Then Sam Houston, with less than 400 men, began a strategic retreat eastward, drawing Santa Anna after him. First Gonzales, then San Felipe, went up in smoke. Women, children, the old and infirm, struggled on foot or in creaking oxcarts through rain, slush, and mire across swollen rivers. Some reached the Trinity, some the Sabine. Bedsheets spread for tents dotted the Louisiana shore. At last, on April 21, Santa Anna, who had dashed on with a fraction of his army to Galveston Bay, hoping to catch (and hang) the officers of the upstart Texas Republic, was surprised by Houston's smaller force on the San Jacinto River, just east of the present city of Houston. The Mexican commander was captured, and more than half his men were killed. The cry was "Remember the Alamo!"

Charles Ramsdell of Austin is an outstanding authority on Texas history. He is a great-grandson of the Mrs. Dickinson who was in the Alamo and was captured when it fell. A former newspaperman and now a free-lance writer, Mr. Ramsdell is the author of San Antonio: A Historical and Pictorial Guide, *and is currently at work on a history of his state.*

fessor Josiah L. Tuck. But no contracts followed. Holland was deeply discouraged. Captain Simpson had been right: it was indeed "very uphill work to put anything through in Washington." To an interviewer he said, with some heat: "So you have sought me as an authority on submarines? Go down to Washington, and you will find plenty of people there who will tell you I know nothing about the subject, nothing at all."

Nevertheless, his friends were steadfast. Kimball urged him on, and warm support came from Charles A. Morris, an engineer who employed Holland in his dredging company from 1891 to 1893; and so far as the Navy was concerned, the times were in Holland's favor. A notable period of experimentation had set in, both in Europe and America, which was to bring the submarine safely to its first maturity.

In Europe Nordenfeldt and an Englishman, G. W. Garrett, were selling their large submarines—64 feet long and displacing 60 tons—to Turkey, Greece, and Russia. France's little electric Goubets of the 1880's had been succeeded by the giant 148-foot *Gustave Zédé*, while in Spain the 70-foot, electrically-operated *Peral* had been launched in 1888. In this country, Congress was becoming aroused, and the submarine was becoming a public issue. Simon Lake had begun to experiment with a submarine, designed for underwater salvage work, which submerged on an even keel instead of diving, and Tuck had also produced an experimental craft. In 1893 there was another competition. Again Holland won. At last, in 1895, the Navy signed its first submarine contract, for $150,000. The contractor: the John P. Holland Torpedo Boat Company, formed by Holland and a young lawyer named Elihu B. Frost.

Some idea of the kind of enthusiasm that Kimball and his friends stirred up in the Navy Department appears in the testimony before a Senate committee about that time by Captain Alfred Thayer Mahan, the country's foremost naval expansionist. "In our present unprotected condition," said Mahan, "the risk of losing the money by the government by reason of the [Holland] boat's being a failure is more than counterbalanced by the great protection the boat would be if a substantial success." And Rear Admiral James E. Jouett testified: "If I commanded a squadron that was

GENERAL DYNAMICS

PIONEERS UNDER THE SEA

When Jules Verne's *Twenty Thousand Leagues Under the Sea* appeared in 1869, it helped advance beyond the realm of dreams an idea which had been in the minds of men for well over a thousand years.

Alexander of Macedon is reputed to have used underwater divers at the siege of Troy in 334 B.C. At about the same time, we are told, he had a glass barrel built (left), in which he had himself lowered to the bottom of the sea "to defy the whale." But the first account of underwater craft which has the ring of authenticity is dated 1505. Olaus Magnus, Bishop of Uppsala in Sweden, tells of seeing in the cathedral of Asloe two "leathern boats" used by pirates of "Gruntland" to attack merchant ships from the surface or from beneath it.

These and a few other submarines recorded over the next two hundred-odd years were all prologue to the serious work of the last three decades of the eighteenth century, when three remarkable inventors were at work: an Englishman named Day (history has nowhere recorded his first name)

blockading a port, and the enemy had half a dozen of these Holland submarine boats, I would be compelled to abandon the blockade and put to sea to avoid destruction of my ships from an invisible source, from which I could not defend myself." Impressed, Congress hastened to appropriate $300,000 for two more Holland boats, should the first one prove successful.

But that first Navy boat, the *Plunger*, was a fiasco from the start. She was built at the Columbian Iron Works in Baltimore. During a good part of the time she was under construction Holland was sick, and the project fell into the hands of naval engineers who knew a good deal less about submarines than he. Unrealistic Navy specifications calling for 1,500 horsepower on the surface and 70 submerged—the *Plunger* was supposed to be capable of a six-hour run at eight knots—resulted in a cumbersome monster 84 feet long. Along with the diving planes which Holland favored, she was equipped with two small down-haul blades in open hatches fore and aft, designed to hold her on an even keel while submerged. Port and starboard main propellers, coupled to a pair of triple-expansion steam engines, drove the submarine on the surface. To propel her underwater she had a third screw, on the axis of the vessel and aft of the rudders, driven by a 75-horsepower electric motor. An additional compound steam engine operated the dynamo used to charge the batteries. She carried two torpedo tubes in the bow.

The *Plunger* was, to put it mildly, over-engineered. Holland, dismayed by what he had brought forth, suggested alterations in the direction of simplicity, but instead the Navy supervisors insisted upon more "improvements" which merely made matters worse. Launched at her dock in 1897, the *Plunger* was so unstable that when her engines were started she nearly turned turtle. When the hatches were closed, moreover, the heat from the huge oil-burning boiler in the center of the boat was so intense that it threatened to cook the crew alive. Attempts were made through 1900 to rehabilitate the boat with a diesel engine, but eventually she was abandoned.

Long before the *Plunger* was finished, Holland realized she would be a dismal failure, but he knew too that further Navy contracts depended on his producing a successful submarine. "The Lord only knows," he wrote, "when [the Navy] will consent to be satisfied to recommend the construction of other boats." Consequently, he persuaded his backers—among them Mrs. Isaac Lawrence of New York, who came up with $25,000—to finance another submarine of his own design. If the Navy wouldn't buy it, at least it could be used as a demonstrator or sold abroad.

and two Americans, David Bushnell and Robert Fulton.

Day's diving vessel (right)—it was no submarine but, oddly enough, a sloop—contained an airtight, watertight chamber and carried thirty tons of stone ballast. When the day of its test came, in June of 1774 in Plymouth Sound, thirty tons proved insufficient to force the boat underwater, and Day had more stones heaved in until the sloop started to sink. He forgot one thing: he would have no way of disposing of the extra stones from his position inside the chamber. Once he had submerged, there was no way of communicating with Mr. Day.

An acquaintance, Dr. N. D. Falck, was in London at the time and reasoned that as long as Day was inside the chamber, preserved by the underwater cold and inaccessible to hungry fish, he had a good chance of being resuscitated. Accordingly the good Doctor removed himself at leisure to Plymouth in July and put in motion a rescue program which continued, without result, until October. Then the weather turned bad, and, as Falck noted, "My private affairs required my attention at home." He went back to London, expecting to return to Plymouth to bring up the unfortu-

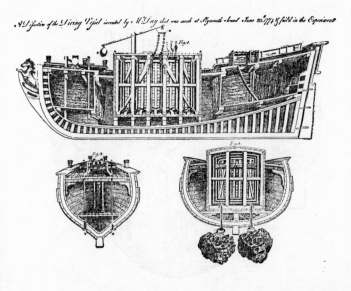
A Section of the Diving Vessel invented by M.* Day that was sunk at Plymouth board June 20, 1774 & faild in the Experiment

With a sense of urgency, Holland sat down at his drafting board, and by September of 1896, when the plans were finished he wrote, with the ardor of an inventor who knows he's on the right track: "I don't think I can improve on the arrangement or general features of this design . . . it represents a powerful and effective boat."

And so it did. Designed in accordance with Holland's belief that "a submarine boat should be as small as possible consistently with possessing sufficient offensive powers," the *Holland* measured only 53.3 feet compared to the *Plunger*'s 84, but would make seven knots submerged and eight on the surface. Moreover, she had a surface cruising range of about 1,000 miles. She was armed with only one torpedo tube—the *Plunger* had two—and two inclined dynamite guns; inside her cramped interior there was room for a crew of five. Like the *Plunger*, she was to have had a steam plant to propel her on the surface, and an electric motor for subsurface running, but when Holland observed at an exhibition in New York a 45-horsepower gasoline engine, he substituted that for the steam plant, retaining the battery-operated electric motor for running underwater.

Thus it was that the following May, at her husband's shipyard in Elizabethport, New Jersey, Mrs. Lewis Nixon appeared in her best brown dress to christen the *Holland* with a bottle of champagne. There were still many details to be attended to after the launching, however, and not until early in 1898 was the *Holland* ready for testing.

By that time the Cuban situation was boiling up toward war, and when, on February 24, the *Holland* headed down Arthur Kill to her first base at Perth Amboy, New Jersey, conflicting rumors began to circulate. One said that the inventor had sold his boat to Cuba, another that he was about to attack the Spanish warship *Vizcaya*, then anchored in New York Harbor. A Navy tug followed carefully that February day, and the next morning the *New York Times* quite seriously reported: "Spanish spies watched the *Holland* from docks above and below the shipyards all the morning."

About the *Holland*'s performance during her early voyages her chief engineer, Charles A. Morris, was exultant. "She goes like a fish," he said, "and dives better than one." But the *Holland*'s first successful dive ended in a mudbank, and the trials were to go on and on. In Raritan Bay on April 20, with an official Navy Board of Inspection looking on, the *Holland* made impressive dives of thirty-eight and fifty-eight minutes, and satisfactorily fired both a dummy aerial pro-

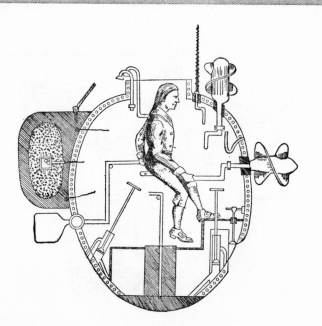

nate Mr. Day; but he never did. Nor was Day ever found.

In the summer of 1776 David Bushnell of Connecticut launched the first true submarine (left) of which we have real knowledge. Called the *Turtle* because it looked like two turtle shells fastened together and floating tail down in the water, it was just large enough to hold a man and the simple instruments necessary for its manipulation.

One night in August, 1776, in New York harbor, the *Turtle* was towed out as far as safety permitted, the hatch was closed, and an Army volunteer named Ezra Lee began the lonely task of cranking the *Turtle*, by means of her screw propellers, toward an unsuspecting British fleet. Most of the way he traveled on the surface, but when he reached the *Eagle*, the enemy flagship, Lee changed to the diving propeller and pressed down the pedals which let water ballast into the boat. He went under the *Eagle* and tried to screw into her bottom an auger connected with a magazine to be exploded by clockwork. But the auger would not go in, and in trying to move to another part of the *Eagle*'s hull, Lee lost contact with his intended victim altogether. The *Turtle* made two more attacks on British shipping, but both failed.

jectile and a dummy torpedo. The Navy, however, downgrading a favorable report from its board, still dragged its feet. The boat had been offered to the government for the war, which began the day after the April trials, but the offer was rejected by the brass despite Secretary of the Navy Theodore Roosevelt's recommendation. The *Holland* never saw action; instead, from a new base in Brooklyn, she continued to undergo tests in the peaceful waters of New York Harbor, occasionally giving demonstration rides to American officers like Kimball and to naval observers from Norway and Japan.

More trials were held in November, this time before a review board including Captain Robley ("Fighting Bob") Evans of Santiago fame. Although everybody was impressed when the *Holland* fired a real Whitehead torpedo, the boat when submerged yawed "like a drunken washerwoman," and the board recommended further trials. Something had to be done about her steering. It was Engineer Morris who finally persuaded Holland that the rudders would have to be repositioned aft of the propeller if she were to answer to her helm. (Morris could hardly envisage the enormous power that was to make the original arrangement work in the nuclear submarine *Skipjack*.) An entrepreneur named Isaac Rice, sold on submarines after a demonstration ride in the *Holland*, paid for the alterations, which were carried out during the winter of 1898–1899. The stern was rebuilt, weight compensation tanks added, and the after dynamite gun removed as superfluous.

In June of 1899 the *Holland*, now operating for Rice's new Electric Boat Company, was towed to Long Island, where the country's first submarine base was established at the Goldsmith and Tuthill yard at New Suffolk. By July a safe, uncrowded three-mile course had been marked out in deserted Little Peconic Bay, and there, removed from a too-inquisitive public, intensive testing was continued during the summer. Occasionally, exhibition runs were made for important people like Clara Barton, founder of the American Red Cross, who scolded Holland roundly for inventing a "deadly instrument of war." Another time, two visiting senators and the crew were temporarily felled by exhaust fumes; the submarine glided into its basin with no one at the controls. In November final, stringent trials, more elaborate than anything that had gone before, were held before another Navy board. Though the boat and its crew acquitted themselves magnificently, the board still turned in an adverse report to Washington.

"We are going to send the *Holland* to Washington

Robert Fulton of Pennsylvania arrived in France in 1797, proposing to build for the French a submarine for use in their war against England. His *Nautilus* (right) was a twenty-one-foot, three-man boat propelled underwater by a crank-operated screw and on the surface by a collapsible sail. Like the *Turtle*, the *Nautilus* carried an explosive fastened to a spike that could be attached to enemy warships.

The *Nautilus* was successfully tested several times, but Fulton and the French could not come to a satisfactory financial arrangement, and he had her broken up for scrap. The inventor, playing both sides of the Channel, then made overtures to England, but Nelson's great victory at Trafalgar ended British interest in exotic weapons. Fulton found his own government similarly unreceptive, and gave his attention henceforward to the steamboat, with which he was successful at last.

—*Lila Parrish Lyman*

The work of Bushnell and Fulton, together with further experiments during the Civil War, set the stage for John Holland and for some of his contemporaries whose designs are shown on the next page.—Ed.

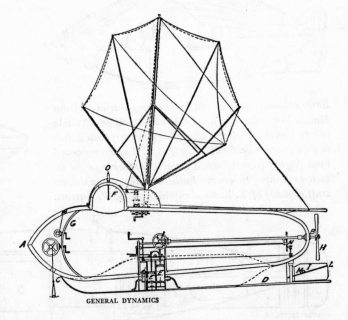

GENERAL DYNAMICS

and make her lobby for an appropriation," an angry Elihu Frost told Kimball. Congress, perhaps, would change the Navy's mind. In December, under Cable's charge, the *Holland* headed down the inland waterway—no insurance company would insure her for a voyage on the open Atlantic—toward the capital.

It was a 500-mile trip, longer than a submarine had ever traveled up to that time. The public was excited. Headlines announced: THE HOLLAND BOAT COMING TODAY; THE HOLLAND BOAT HERE. Crowds lined the banks of the canals and mobbed the boat wherever she tied up. Arriving in Washington, the *Holland* was overhauled at the navy yard during the winter, and between March 14 and 27, 1900, final Navy trials were held on the Potomac. An enthusiastic Admiral Dewey watched the first run (his aide, Lieutenant Harry H. Caldwell, was in the boat). While the *Holland* awaited the Navy's verdict, exhibitions were held for newspapermen, foreign naval attachés, and congressmen. On April 11 the Navy finally agreed to purchase the *Holland*, and accepted her a week later. The price was $150,000. She had cost $236,615 to build.

That summer the boat, under command of Lieutenant Caldwell and a Navy crew, made headlines as well as history by officially "sinking" several large warships while on trial maneuvers with the fleet off New-

port. She was commissioned on October 12. Thereafter she sank into obscurity, serving for many years as a submarine trainer before being stricken from the lists in 1910. But her work had been done. Hard on her heels came the seven boats of the *Holland*-type "A class," the Navy's first submarine fleet, while similar craft were built for the fleets of England and Japan. The submarine at last had gained some recognition from the great powers.*

As for John Holland himself, he was inevitably pushed aside as the Electric Boat Company, under Rice's guidance, developed into an established concern. Frost, who had helped Holland form his own company not many years before, turned against him. Later there were serious differences over the design of the A class, and the engineering staff began to ignore the old man as far as they dared. Holland, who had never

* The little *Holland* in her old age was exhibited in several cities; then in 1930 was purchased for $100 from a park in the Bronx and ignominiously scrapped. The *Plunger* suffered a similar fate; but the *Fenian Ram* survives in Paterson's Westside Park, thanks to the generosity of a native of Paterson who as a boy had been kindly treated by Holland. (The inventor loved children, his daughter relates, because "they were the only ones who didn't think he was crazy!") As for Boat No. 1, it was dug out of the mud of the Passaic River in 1927 and can now be viewed in the Paterson Museum.

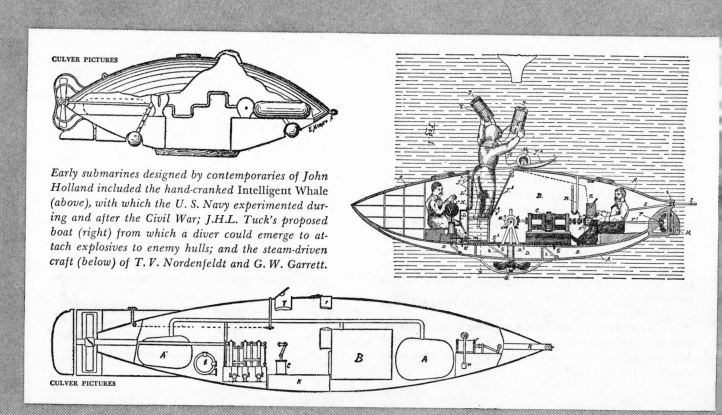

CULVER PICTURES

Early submarines designed by contemporaries of John Holland included the hand-cranked Intelligent Whale *(above), with which the U. S. Navy experimented during and after the Civil War; J.H.L. Tuck's proposed boat (right) from which a diver could emerge to attach explosives to enemy hulls; and the steam-driven craft (below) of T. V. Nordenfeldt and G. W. Garrett.*

CULVER PICTURES

trusted those who had taken over his invention, left the firm in 1904 and tried to set up in business for himself.

He built two boats for Japan that year, receiving the Order of the Rising Sun from a grateful Nipponese government. In 1905, having designed an ocean-going submarine faster than the Fleet-type boats that would appear in World War II, he formed a new company and tried to interest the Navy. But the Electric Boat Company, fighting for its life, scared away his capital with legal actions and blocked him at every turn. The Navy's rejection of his new boat in 1907 was curt and final.

Nevertheless, he had built soundly. The little *Holland* set a high standard for the future, and her basic mechanisms and principles were carried over into the submarines of every navy. Unlike the important early submarines of Lake and Nordenfeldt, with their "even keel" method of submerging, the *Holland* dove like a porpoise. She maintained a "reserve buoyancy" and was forced or steered underwater, while in motion, by her stern diving rudders and propeller. An immovable center of gravity, along with compensation for any loss of internal weight by use of trimming tanks, kept the boat at all times in fine adjustment of balance and weight. The *Holland* was the first submarine to employ the combination of an internal-combustion engine for surface running and an electric motor for submerged work, setting a firm precedent for the future.

The submarine as it developed through World War II, however, became so heavy and complex both in operation and design that much of the agile simplicity of Holland's original conception was lost. The large Fleet type, for instance, was in reality a fast, long-range, diesel-powered *surface* craft capable of submerging for only relatively short distances at a much slower speed. Its ratio of twenty-one knots on the surface to nine submerged was in sharp contrast to the Holland's remarkable eight to seven. Nevertheless, it was an effective weapon. Even its World War I predecessor, in German hands, very nearly broke the British blockade of the Fatherland. In World War II, U-boats made the efforts of the United States to supply its European allies a difficult and deadly dangerous business. And the American Fleet-type submarine effectively cut Japan's home islands off from its Pacific outposts of empire.

Right after the war came atomic power, first used in the *Nautilus*. Radar had forced the submarine below the surface to avoid detection. With atomic power it could now stay there, where it belonged, for almost indefinite periods. The result has been a high compliment to Holland's genius: a return, in the recent *Skip-*

jack class, to the efficient, whale-like configuration, the single screw astern of the rudders, and the one-man control which had been typical of the original Holland design.

Though his submarines lacked the power and size of these modern giants, Holland had created something close to the "true submersible"—the ideal of today. "Why, you could spit across the *Holland*," exclaimed old Roger Williams, once a member of the little boat's Navy crew, when he was shown the great bulk of the *Nautilus* in 1955. But Andrew McKee, chief designer for General Dynamics' Electric Boat Division at Groton, builder of many of the nuclear-powered craft, has observed that the modern submarine is beginning to look suspiciously like the *Holland*. Size is unimportant: the design is everything.

That final Navy rejection in 1907, however, had broken the spirit of a proud and gifted man. Rheumatism plagued Holland's final years. "Unknown to his neighbors as a man of any note," wrote an associate, Frank T. Cable, "he lived in East Orange, New Jersey, his small frame stooping, his gait awkward, his manner nervous due to his nearsightedness, which increased with the years, yet keen-brained, studious, and ambitious to the last . . ." He spent much time in a workshop at the rear of his home—it was "sealed with various locks," Cable remembered—where he designed and built the aeronautical devices that had fascinated him ever since he was a young teacher in Ireland. He would walk out with his old comrade, Kimball, to study the flight of birds. "Many an hour have I held a stop watch on great gulls, frigate birds, booby birds and albatross," Kimball recalled, "trying to get data for Holland." In 1912 the old Irish patriot emerged briefly from retirement—to warn England's First Lord of the Admiralty against the growing submarine menace. He died, almost unnoticed, on August 12, 1914; a month later the submarine first showed its deadly might when a German U-boat sank three British cruisers with the loss of 1,370 lives.

It was Kimball who wrote John Holland's epitaph: "He was a fair fighter," the Admiral said, "a most interesting and amusing companion, the staunchest of friends. God rest his soul."

Richard K. Morris, a grandson of the Holland's *first engineer, Charles A. Morris, teaches at Trinity College in Hartford, Connecticut, and is at work on a biography of John P. Holland. Courtlandt Canby of New York was co-editor of the recently published* Dynamic America, *an illustrated history of the General Dynamics Corporation, and is the author of* Lincoln and the Civil War. *He is editor of* The Epic of Man, *to be published next year by* Life.

appointment. "What the hell is he doing on this mission?"

With Robins, there entered upon the stage a figure who was to prove the one brilliant, although short-lived, star in a cast of many-colored American principals in Russia. For principals they all were, each man regarding himself the direct representative of the President by virtue of blessing or laying-on of hands, and thus responsible first to the White House, second to his own conscience and beliefs, and to the ambassador on the spot not at all—a situation that President Wilson did nothing to resolve. The ebullient Thompson, setting himself up in high style in Petrograd and taking over the imperial box at the Opera, reported directly to Washington and did not even show the unhappy Francis his cables; thus, when Thompson donated a million rubles' worth of his own money to the moderate Social-Revolutionary party, Ambassador Francis learned of this startling American involvement only through the newspapers. Nor did General Judson, busily maneuvering in the revolutionary murk at the head of his own independent military mission, confide in the Ambassador; while Edgar Sisson too, a small man inflated by a sense of sovereign responsibility, was to write proudly of *his* mission to Petrograd, "I was not sent to work under [Francis], and was independent of him, in powers and in funds."

In this chaos of unco-ordinated equals, the municipal reformer from Chicago was to stand out by the sheer intensity of his personality as America's strongest man on the scene. Although submerged in memory today, Raymond Robins was in 1917 a famous figure in the liberal camp at home. His physical presence itself was commanding: broad-shouldered, deep-chested, square-jawed, with intense, searching eyes and a rasping, emotional voice that could carry away whole convention halls of reformers. He had been the Progressive party's keynoter in 1916 and had run for the Senate. Yet there was something else in him, too—a suggestion of mystical exaltation that thrilled some followers and left others thinking him slightly unbalanced.

A "rough and ready evangelist," Sisson called him, and something of his passionate reformist spirit now communicated itself to Russia's far-left revolutionaries. They were not used to this: their own followers had been reared rigidly according to the gospel of St. Marx. Yet they were all still young in exercise of power, and not yet so calloused by it as to denounce every non-Marxist reformer as an enemy; and so, responding to the

warmth and virility of Robins' presence, they saw in him a bridge—perhaps the only bridge—between their erupting Russia and the capitalist West. And Robins, whose experience was also limited but whose sympathies were broad, responded in kind. As his British friend and opposite number as London's special agent in Russia, R. H. Bruce Lockhart, was to remark,

[Robins] was an Indian chief with a Bible for his tomahawk. . . . Yet, in spite of his sympathies for the underdog, he was a worshipper of great men . . . Strangely enough, Lenin was amused by the hero-worship, and of all foreigners Robins was the only man whom Lenin was always willing to see and who ever succeeded in imposing his personality on the unemotional Bolshevik leader.

So it happened that while David Francis remained closeted in the Furshtatskaya over cards, American initiative in dealing with the new rulers of Russia passed into the hands of this assimilated lieutenant colonel of the Red Cross.

All during the autumn of 1917, the unlikely combination of Thompson and Robins had worked together to succor the weakening Kerensky regime with money, foodstuffs, and propaganda placed in judiciously subsidized newspapers. But in mid-October Robins read the handwriting on Russia's wall and called for a change in our own response. The Provisional regime was doomed amid the rising cry of "Peace, Bread, and Land," he argued, unless Kerensky at once proceeded to distribute land to the peasants and launch other major social reforms. It should be America's new policy to exert pressure on all Russian moderates to move in this direction, he went on, if the Bolsheviks were not to take over at any moment and pull Russia out of the war altogether. Also, Robins thought it might be a good idea at least to talk with these Bolshevik chieftains, size them up, and discover whether we could influence them at all.

Then in October-November, the second and greater revolutionary storm in Russia broke out—just as Robins had predicted it would. The multimillionaire Thompson, finding himself in full agreement with his deputy's analysis, sped home to Washington to try to swing the Administration onto a new policy tack—only to find himself coolly rebuffed by Wilson, who was still reading David Francis' bland cables and who now refused to let himself be jolted. Meanwhile, in Petrograd, the headstrong Colonel Robins had taken it upon himself to approach Trotsky personally—and Lenin too.

In order to reach Trotsky, the Foreign Commissar of a regime the United States declined to recognize, Robins needed an intermediary. Soon he found one in the person of Alexander Gumberg, a squat, mournful-looking, shrewd Jewish Russo-American who had emigrated to the Bronx to become manager there of the Russian-language Socialist weekly, *Novy Mir,* to which Trotsky had contributed during his own American exile. Now returned to his old country to be close to his Socialist friends in action, Gumberg became Robins' personal aide—and threw open the Bolshevik leader's doors to him.

When Robins drove to the Smolny Institute in mid-November for his first meeting with Trotsky, he was still convinced, as were most of the other Americans in Petrograd, that the Commissar was in effect a German agent, bent on creating total upheaval in the Allied camp and on delivering a shattered Russia into the hands of Hindenburg and Ludendorff. When he came away, he had reversed his opinion. Trostky, he later said, with the emotionalism typical of him, was indeed a ". . . son of a bitch, but the greatest Jew since Jesus Christ. If the German General Staff bought Trotsky, they bought a lemon."

"I won Trotsky," Robins recalled, "by putting my case absolutely on the square. By not hiding anything." He told Trotsky that he was there because he wanted to deal with those in power, that he wanted to maintain Red Cross activities in Russia, that he wanted to keep Russia in the war, and that he wanted to know plainly whether the Bolsheviks' sympathies were on the side of Germany or not. Trotsky, evidently astonished by this forthright approach, convinced his visitor that he was as anxious as Robins himself to keep vital war supplies out of the hands of the oncoming German legions, and on the spot worked out an arrangement with him to safeguard some essential stocks.

Soon after, though, Trotsky began commuting between the Smolny and the wintry waste of occupied Brest-Litovsk, in search of a separate peace with Germany—negotiations that, in Allied eyes, were an infamous betrayal. Could anything be salvaged from the wreckage? Robins still hoped so. It was now January, 1918, and there was no time to lose. At any moment the Germans, if sure of victory on their eastern front, might begin mounting a fresh onslaught in the west.

"We have started peace negotiations with the Germans," Trotsky told Robins flatly. "We have asked the Allies to join us in starting peace negotiations for the whole world, on a democratic basis—no forcible annexations, no punitive indemnities, and a full acceptance of the principle of the self-determination of all peoples. The Allies have refused to accept our invitation. We still hope, of course, to compel them."

The Progressive gazed at the Commissar. "How?"

"By stirring up comrades in France and in England and in America to upset the policy of their governments by asserting their own revolutionary socialist will. . . . Germany will want a peace with annexations. *But we have these raw materials.* Germany needs them. If we can keep them away from Germany we have an argument in reserve, a big argument, perhaps a winning argument."

"I begin to see," said Robins.

The long-haired, bespectacled revolutionist ground on. "I want to keep them away, but you know our difficulties at the front. The front is in chaos. Send your officers, American officers, Allied officers, any officers you please. I will give them full authority to enforce the embargo against goods into Germany all along our whole front."

Which was it, then: were these new Russian masters sworn enemies of ours or still, despite all differences, potential allies against German domination? General Judson, after quiet talks on his own at the Smolny, agreed with Robins: by recognizing them and showing them sympathy, we could keep Russia in the war and influence it in victory. (Back home, Thompson was saying to anyone who would listen, "Let's make them *our* Bolsheviks.") Ambassador Francis, on the other hand, after one brief moment of illumination in which he too agreed that we might do well to recognize the new rulers in order to revive Russia's role in the war, returned to regarding them as foes beyond the pale; and in late December he encouraged his consul general at Moscow, the aristocratically connected Maddin Summers, to send an emissary to make contact with the counterrevolutionary White Russians gathering in the northern provinces—a move sure to bring about further enmity once the Soviets learned of it.

Very briefly, at the end of the year, a pale sun of possible Russo-American reconciliation rose over the wintry Neva. The Germans' territorial demands on Russia proved so outrageous that negotiations at Brest-Litovsk came near breaking down. On December 31, agog with excitement at the thought that Bolshevik Russia might yet resume the fight against Germany, Robins rushed to the Smolny to confront Trotsky. Then Trotsky asked him point-blank: What support could America give to Soviet Russia if it turned down the Germans' terms and thus re-entered the war? This, until the events of World War II, was perhaps the most formidable question asked of America in a crucial time—and Trotsky had to ask it of a man whom Francis described as a "wild Indian," and who could of course give him no authoritative answer.

One answer from the very summit did come, though,

stimulated in part by another man on the spot: Edgar Sisson. Aware with Robins of the parlous state of American relations with Russia, Sisson on January 3 cabled his chief at the Committee on Public Information in Washington, George Creel, to propose that the President issue a statement on American war aims as against those of Germany, with particular reference to the latter's as revealed at Brest-Litovsk, "to . . . open up our opportunities for publicity and helpfulness" in Russia.

Just how directly the Sisson message influenced President Wilson remains a matter of dispute. Five days later, however, there emerged from the White House the famous statement known to history as the "Fourteen Points," calling for many of the same principles in international settlement that Trotsky had aired to Robins. Sisson described its reception in Petrograd:

This time Lenin was back and we [*i.e.,* Sisson, Robins, and Gumberg, with a copy of the translation in hand] were able to get direct to him. It did not take one minute to convince him that the full message should go to Trotsky [who was then again at Brest-Litovsk] by direct wire. He grabbed the copy and sprinted for the telegraph office himself. . . . It was the first time either Robins or myself had met Lenin . . . Lenin, in appearance, might be the *bourgeois* mayor of a French town—short, sparsely bearded, a bronze man in hair and whiskers, small, shrewd eyes, round of face, smiling and genial when he desires to be. And this time he did. But he is the Wildest of the Wild Men of Russia . . . He welcomed the message . . . but he did not let us forget for a moment that he regarded it as coming not from a fellow thinker but from a just and tolerant class opponent.

Yet, while Wilson's Fourteen Points declaration momentarily re-inspirited the Bolsheviks in their idea of resistance, it was not followed up by any move of American recognition or aid, and thus did not affect the grim negotiations for Russian surrender and dismemberment now being resumed at Brest-Litovsk. (The Bolsheviks, for their part, had done their perverse best to reduce any chances of such aid by appropriating two million rubles for the use of their agents to foment world revolution—and publicizing this fact.) Trotsky, who reviled both the Germans and the Allies and who had no effective forces in hand to fight either, save through the deployment of ideas and slogans, hit upon the startling formula in the snows of Brest-Litovsk, "No peace and no war"—meaning that Russia was taking itself entirely out of the international community, refusing to fight, negotiate, or settle. Observers throughout the world were nonplused—none more so than our own in Russia. Sisson, falling out with Robins, said he was sure now that Lenin and Trotsky were playing Germany's game, and he managed to acquire a stack of secret papers that in his opinion proved it. Robins,

on the other hand, kept hoping that as Germany heightened its demands and backed them up with a march on Petrograd, a new fighting spirit among the Russians could yet be kindled—if only we recognized and aided their new chieftains. But his military ally, General Judson, had in the meantime been called home and shelved for "interfering" too much; and Ambassador Francis observed the final day of January, 1918, by breaking out a new stock of bourbon.

The Kaiser's hordes approached the capital, meeting no resistance. The Allied embassies burned their papers and fled to Vologda, a mud-ridden junction town on the railroad line to Archangel. On March 5 Robins had an extraordinary meeting with Lenin and Trotsky, then wavering between surrender and renewed resistance, and the three together drafted an inquiry to the United States government asking what kind of aid might be forthcoming if the Soviets refused to ratify the Brest-Litovsk treaty and resumed fighting. Nine days later Lenin confronted Robins again, just before entering the chamber of his All-Russian Congress of Workmen's, Soldiers', and Peasants' Deputies for the debate on the treaty. "Have you heard from your Government?" he asked.

"No, I've not heard yet."

"Has Lockhart heard from London?"

"Not yet," said Robins, and added, "Couldn't you prolong the debate?"

"The debate must take its course."

Two days later, a final confrontation at the Congress: once more Lenin asked Robins whether a reply had come from Washington. There had been none. Lenin turned away: "I shall now speak for the peace. It will be ratified."

Events thus moved quickly to their denouement. The Soviets ratified. Allied troops landed at Murmansk to protect war materials shipped there in aid of Russia from the West, and then to support White Russians against the regime. In America the sentiment for like armed intervention grew: the Bolsheviks, first dismissed as dim and distant agitators, now took on the image of world-wide ogres in cahoots with the Hun. Francis, an ambassador without an embassy to perform, bestirred himself enough to order that any contacts with the Soviets by General Judson's remaining aides cease. In May, Robins was recalled; Secretary of State Lansing cut him off brusquely, and the President refused to see him. Sisson, for his part, had already slipped quietly out of Russia with his cache of documents purporting to show that Lenin and Trotsky were in the pay of Germany, and these were to be published amid great excitement under the seal of the United States—though many experts, like Lockhart, later held them to be forgeries. In July, Francis himself packed up and left Vologda, thereby ending an American representation in Russia maintained ever since John Quincy Adams had arrived 109 years before; and in July, President Wilson agreed to American armed intervention on Russian soil (*see* "Where Ignorant Armies Clashed by Night," in the December, 1958, AMERICAN HERITAGE).

What had been undone on both sides was never fully to be repaired. As to the actors themselves, Robins, a lost soul, haunted the halls of Congress for a few years, trying to bring about recognition of the Soviets as a means of influencing them, and then dropped from sight. Sisson lived on to become a wizened minor propagandist in the Second World War, still buttonholing people to convince them of the authenticity of his documents. Francis, back in St. Louis with his gramophone, wrote a long book defending all he had done in Petrograd; Gumberg, a Socialist with a sure instinct for adaptation, became a highly paid executive in Wall Street; Trotsky, as everyone knows, met his end under the blow of an axe in Mexico City.

A frequent contributor to AMERICAN HERITAGE, *William Harlan Hale is managing editor of* HORIZON. *He is at present at work on a book about well-known Americans abroad.*

For further reading: George F. Kennan's Russia Leaves the War *(Princeton University Press, 1956) and* The Decision to Intervene *(Princeton University Press, 1958); American Russian Relations, 1781–1947, by William Appleman Williams (Rinehart, 1952); and* The Forgotten Peace, *by John Wheeler-Bennett (William Morrow, 1939).*

In the October, 1960, AMERICAN HERITAGE, *the introduction to "A Soviet View of Six Great Americans" quoted Adlai Stevenson's apt characterization of certain articles in the* Large Soviet Encyclopedia *as a "curiously dehumanized account of history in which a stereotyped pattern of impersonal force supplants individual effort." We regret that through an oversight this remark was credited only to its author and not to its source, the preface of a publication of the State Historical Society of Wisconsin, Madison, entitled* A Soviet View of the American Past, *an annotated translation of another section of the same Russian encyclopedia, its article on American history. Those who enjoyed the article in this magazine will find the Wisconsin pamphlet interesting further reading.*

Penn's City: American Athens

CONTINUED FROM PAGE 13

lacked due representation and participation in the government of affairs, along with still others of strong liberal feelings—gathered in a conference of their own, dismissed the proprietary government, and in the name of all the people instructed their delegates to Congress to vote for independence. No other colony had gone so far as to mix the question of internal reform with the question of its relation to England. Few of the Founding Fathers had come to Philadelphia prepared to acknowledge the principle of popular sovereignty, and the effect on them of this democratic prerevolution was enormous.

We are accustomed to think that no city can be to this nation what Paris, London, and Rome are to their respective countries: the main center, not only of government but of wealth, fashion, population, and intellectual power as well. The explosive growth of the United States in the nineteenth century discouraged any such centralization. Today there are more than half a dozen American cities larger than Washington, each with its separate claim to national distinction, its own urban standards, and its own social pretensions.

But during the formative and critical period of our history, Philadelphia enjoyed a relative importance that no American city can claim today. In the twenty-five years preceding Adams' first visit in 1774, its population had more than tripled, putting it well ahead of both Boston and New York in the race for numbers. From 1774 to 1783 it was the nerve center of the Revolution; from 1790 to 1800 it was the federal capital; and before, during, and after those crucial times it was ornamented by a more urbane and agreeable society—fashionable, literary, and political—than could be found anywhere except in a few European capitals.

That flourishing urban culture was rooted in opulence, as such cultures generally are. Philadelphia had early become a principal market of the Delaware watershed, an area that included the richest and most carefully husbanded land in America; and as the bounty of the countryside poured into the city, the more enterprising and better-placed merchants found wealth dumped into their laps. Devout and high-minded as he was, William Penn had a cultivated taste for the good things of life, which he could usually well afford. In their turn, his most prosperous followers in the citadel of Quakerism cultivated a standard of living that even sophisticated Parisian visitors found luxurious—and unexpected. During the span of years that he lived in Philadelphia, off and on, John Adams never easily reconciled himself to the unpuritanical and lavish hospitality of these "nobles" of Pennsylvania.

Occasionally the social activities reported in his diaries seem to have seriously tried his New England conscience; as on an evening when he had dined with distinguished company at Samuel Powel's "splendid seat" on South Third Street. He recorded "a most sinful feast again! every thing which could delight the eye or allure the taste; curds and creams, jellies, and sweetmeats of various sorts, twenty sorts of tarts, fools, trifles, floating islands, whipped sillabubs &c. &c., Parmesan cheese, punch, wine, porter, beer, &c." But he shortly made the necessary adjustments. Describing another, comparable orgy at the "elegant and most magnificent" home of Benjamin Chew, he concluded his report triumphantly: "I drank Madeira at a great rate, *and found no inconvenience in it.*" A few weeks later (it was at the conclusion of his first visit) he bade adieu to "the happy, the peaceful, the elegant, the hospitable, and polite city of Philadelphia."

It is easy to believe that the social and intellectual climate of Philadelphia had a liberalizing influence, not only on Adams, but on a great many of his contemporaries. In its heyday the city stood at the crossroads of America, both geographically and figuratively. Before the Revolution the best minds of colonial America had been brought to a focus in Philadelphia by the activity of the American Philosophical Society, the oldest and most renowned learned society in the land. The Society not only fed back a synthesis of American intellectual and scientific accomplishment to the colonies but relayed it across the Atlantic to European illuminati, many of whom were glad to accept membership in the Philadelphia Society. The botanical gardens of John Bartram were known to amateur and professional naturalists at home and abroad, including the King of England, the Queen of Sweden, and the scientists of remote Russia. The seeds and specimens Bartram sent overseas to his numerous correspondents were responsible for the naturalization in England alone of more than 150 American plants. For a time Provost Smith edited at Philadelphia the *American Magazine and Monthly Chronicle,* the most brilliant and original colonial periodical, in which he planned, by means of "extensive correspondence with men of learning throughout the colonies" to present to the world an interpretation of the American scene. The publication was discontinued within a year, but through its pages Smith brought to light a group of varied talents that included Francis Hopkinson, the first American composer of secular music; Thomas Godfrey, the first American dramatist to have his work professionally performed; and Benjamin West, possibly the most widely known American painter of all time—not excepting Grandma Moses, Alexander Cal-

der, and Jackson Pollock. In some quarters of the intellectual world, America must have been identified with Philadelphia.

At Princeton in 1771 two young Philadelphia poets hailed their city as the "mistress of our world, the seat of arts, of science, and of fame," an effusion which even a New England almanac of the same year virtually echoed. During the decade before the Revolution, the painters Charles Willson Peale, Matthew Pratt, Henry Benbridge, and Abraham Delanoy all returned from their studies abroad, largely with West, and by their reputations helped to make their city the most active artistic center in the colonies. The prosperous gentry provided abundant patronage, which, in a time when artists were not yet obliged to starve in garrets to prove their genius, made the city a shining goal for painters, portraitists mostly, from other parts. With cynical acumen, an English critic once observed that "wherever the British settle, wherever they colonize, they carry, and will always carry, trial by jury, horse racing, and portrait painting." The latter, he claimed, "is always independent of art and has little or nothing to do with it . . . [portraiture] is one of the staple manufactures of the realm." Be that as it may, in the generation before the Revolution at least three dozen portrait painters found employment for their skills in Philadelphia. As John Singleton Copley, the greatest of them, wrote in 1771, it was "a place of too much importance not to visit."

Returning from his years abroad, Thomas Jefferson thought that Philadelphia was a handsomer city than either London or Paris. The neat symmetry of the city, indeed, excited comment from almost every visitor. Its broad, straight, paved, and tree-lined streets were to the eighteenth century an agreeable novelty in themselves, as were its innumerable and ever-gushing water pumps. Carpenters' Hall, the handsome little home of the Carpenters' Company and the meeting place of the First Continental Congress, was headquarters for the master builders and amateur architects who were responsible to a large extent for the solid and impressive constructions with which the city abounded. It was due to the conceptions and skills of these men that Independence Hall with its adjacent buildings, Carpenters' Hall included, developed into the first civic center and the most delightful urban complex in America.

For his numerous contributions to the city's development one of this group, Robert Smith, an immigrant Quaker "mechanick" from Glasgow, came to be known as the "Architect of Philadelphia"; he was a zealous member of the American Philosophical Society, and in his city home and his country place he enjoyed most of the comforts and pursued the same social satisfactions that made life agreeable for his wealthiest patrons. This sort of well-rounded fulfillment was probably more easily attainable by a working craftsman in Philadelphia than anywhere else in the colonies. The elder Samuel Powel, father of Adams' host, was another member of the Carpenters' Company who won honor through his craft as "a Man remarkable for his Care in promoting Regularity in the Buildings of Philadelphia" and who also amassed a considerable fortune. Although the younger Samuel never had to work, he too was a member of the Company. Just before his return from Europe, his uncle felt obliged to remind him that the artisans of Philadelphia were the peers of the English, and that the joiners of the city might be ill-pleased if Powel brought back with him furniture made abroad. He did so, but he still remained popular enough to be chosen as Philadelphia's last pre-Revolutionary mayor.

The high life of the city—its dancing assemblies and concerts, its fishing parties on the Schuylkill, its cock fights and other worldly diversions—were hardly interrupted by the Revolution. The exclusive Schuylkill Fishing Company of the State in Schuylkill did, in a splendid patriotic gesture, deed back to the United States the complete extraterritorial rights it had secured from colonial governors (a gesture it lived to regret during prohibition days). But during the time of the British occupation, the "heavenly, sweet, pretty redcoats" (as the Tory belles viewed the invaders) gave a ball—the famous Mischianza—of such size and splendor it is still talked about in Philadelphia. After the British quit the city and before hostilities had altogether ceased, the French minister, to celebrate the birth of the Dauphin, presented an entertainment that made even the Mischianza seem modest. "Indeed," wrote a German visitor to Philadelphia in 1783, "the long sojourn of many foreigners, military men and others, has greatly changed manners, tastes, and ideas, widening and increasing a disposition for all pleasures."

In April, 1790, the entire civilized world turned its attention briefly to Philadelphia as it mourned the death of Franklin, the man who had been recognized even more widely than Washington as a symbol of America. Later that year, when the federal government moved down from New York, Washington himself became Philadelphia's first citizen. Concerned lest he should seem to derive the slightest personal advantage from his position, he rented and furnished at his own expense the house of Robert Morris, agreeing among other things to keep the mangle for ironing clothes that Mrs. Morris had chosen to leave behind only if his own mangle proved to be "*equally* good and convenient" and acceptable to Mrs. Morris in exchange. John Adams, first as Vice President and later as Chief Executive, was equally scrupulous, and had a miserable time accommodating his notions of domestic economy to the high price of living in Philadelphia. As long as he was given "so despicable an allowance," he wrote his wife in 1793, he would never live at the seat of government "but at lodgings." "Shiver my jib and start my planks if I do," he added emphatically.

Those last ten years of the century were the most brilliant in the city's history. The formal weekly levees of the President, and his wife's somewhat more spirited receptions, naturally attracted the city's most distinguished and ambitious company. Now that it was the seat of the "republican court," the city seemed to have gone half mad and altogether prodigal in its zest for social entertainment. The indisputable leader of this society, which for wit, taste, and brilliant worldliness has never been surpassed in America, was the beautiful, gracious, enormously wealthy Mrs. William Bingham. Young Charles Bulfinch, on his way to becom-

Drawn from memory by C.A. Poulson

Typical of Philadelphia's fine houses during its golden age were Robert Morris' (right) at Sixth and Market, and George Washington's next door.

105

Carpenters' Hall in 1774.

ing New England's most prominent and fashionable architect, thought that with its "white marble staircase, valuable paintings, the richest furniture and the utmost magnificence of decoration," the Bingham establishment was "far *too rich* for *any* man in this country." Here and at Lansdowne, her country seat, her entertainments reached a level of luxury and urbanity hitherto unknown to America.

This gracious hostess, whom Abigail Adams conceded was the finest woman she had ever seen—surpassing the celebrated Duchess of Devonshire in charm and beauty, had the name of each guest at her parties called by a servant at the entrance, to be picked up by another on the stairs, and relayed in a loud voice to a third servant at the door to the drawing room. On his first exposure to this imported formality, James Monroe, hearing his name repeated so insistently, is said to have called back, "Coming—coming, as soon as I get my greatcoat off."

As the metropolis of a new "empire," the city became something of an international capital. Besides foreign diplomatic personnel, there were curious tourists who came to see at close range this novel experiment in republican government, which Frederick the Great said could not possibly survive as such, which Turgot hailed as "the hope of the human race," and which, much later, seemed to H. G. Wells so fresh and unblemished that he likened it to "something coming out of an egg." French émigrés converged on Philadelphia in successive waves following each change of authority in revolutionary France and its colonies. Some, among them even the most distinguished, came as refugees, and the city was treated to the curious spectacle of French counts teaching fencing to Quaker lads and dancing to Quaker lasses to make a living (Chateaubriand reported that even the Iroquois tribe had a French dancing master, a M. Violet). Moreau de Saint-Méry, sometime *de facto* president of the Commune, ran a bookstore (he also introduced America to contraceptives as a side line to his trade in literature) which became a rendezvous for the Vicomte de Noailles, Comte Rochambeau, the Duc de La Rochefoucauld-Liancourt, the Duc d'Orléans, and other celebrated compatriots. Talleyrand prepared his international intrigues on the shores of the Schuylkill, and Brillat-Savarin, be-

tween fiddling in a theater and teaching French to make ends meet, made notes on the American cuisine, which later appeared in his *Physiologie du Goût*.

The impact of these elegant Parisians on Philadelphia was no greater than the impact of life in Philadelphia on them. A number of them professed to be shocked by the conspicuous luxury of the city. The Duc de La Rochefoucauld-Liancourt referred to entertainments as stylish and splendid as any he had seen in Europe. Brissot de Warville, noting two ladies who came to a formal dinner with "very naked" bosoms, was scandalized by "this indecency among republicans." Moreau de Saint-Méry was intrigued by the local custom of giving houses even-numbered addresses on one side of the street and odd on the other, an idea he introduced to Paris when he returned there. Chastellux observed that here, where all ranks were theoretically equal, men followed their natural bent by giving the preference to riches. The Duc d'Orléans, later the "citizen king" Louis Philippe, but whose future was at that time uncertain, made the mistake of applying this principle by asking for the hand of William Bingham's daughter. With the solid assurance of a Philadelphia aristocrat the young lady's father is said to have replied, "Should you ever be restored to your hereditary position, you will be too great a match for her; if not, she is too great a match for you."

Gilbert Stuart came to Philadelphia in 1794 to start the series of innumerable likenesses of George Washington he was to paint and to establish himself immediately as "court painter" and America's foremost portraitist. He was an inimitable raconteur, an audacious wag, and his Chestnut Street quarters became as much a salon as a studio. In later years he enjoyed badgering his fellow Bostonians by recalling the days he spent in "the Athens of America," and the Spartans of the North had to suffer his barbs. Massachusetts was at the time still in what Charles Francis Adams, a century later, called its "glacial period," and for a while yet Philadelphia remained the nation's cultural capital.

Thomas Jefferson was too much of a radical (as Franklin had been too much of a plebian) to be warmly welcomed by the elite of Philadelphia society. But he found the city beautiful, and rich in intellectual companionship as well. Franklin's old friend Joseph Priestley, "inventor" of oxygen, had fled to Philadelphia from the wrath of Tory mobs in England, and Jefferson discussed with him plans for a new American university. Another of Franklin's friends, the incomparable self-taught mathematician and astronomer David Rittenhouse, was the current president of the American Philosophical Society. Of his famous orrery, the planetarium of the day, Jefferson observed, "He has not, indeed, made a world, but he has by imitation approached nearer its Maker than any man who has lived, from the creation to this day."

William Bartram, who presided over his father's botanical gardens, within a short walk from Jefferson's residence, did not create a world either. But with his volume of American travels, published in 1791, he provided a vision of the New World that profoundly impressed his own generation and those to come. His scientific and poetic description of the American scene as he had viewed it in all its colorful variety was a literary masterpiece of early romanticism, and to its pages Coleridge, Southey, Chateaubriand, and Wordsworth turned to inform their speculations about the world in general and America in particular.

A generation ago one of Christopher Morley's Main Line heroes told his girl that Philadelphia "had her spell of modernism and revolution in the eighteenth century and got through with it once and for all." That was not strictly true. For several decades after the national capital moved on to Washington in 1800, Philadelphia remained the creative focus of American art. Here American painting graduated from its colonial phase into full-fledged artistic activity with professional organization, a transition in which Charles Willson Peale played a parental role. As a craftsman, an artist, and a man of indefatigable curiosity, Peale seemed able to work out every idea that came to him. He had organized the first art school, which held a public exhibit as early as 1795. Ten years later the Pennsylvania Academy of Fine Arts was organized as the first successful public institution devoted to art. Peale's own museum, with all the oddities included in its collections, remained one of the major cultural institutions in the United States for several decades to come, until it was finally vulgarized into a pre-Barnum side show.

Perhaps the best proof of the stored-up vitality of the city was its position as the foremost publishing center of the nation, an eminence it retained at least until the third decade of the nineteenth century. Philadelphia already had to her credit the first American edition of Shakespeare and the first American anthology. In 1807 *The Columbiad* of Joel Barlow, a New Englander, was published there—a book hailed as "in all respects the finest specimen of bookmaking ever produced . . . by an American press." Between times, Philadelphia had given the world the novels of Charles Brockden Brown, the nation's first professional novelist, now all but forgotten but hailed by Keats and Shelley as a "powerful genius" comparable to the renowned Schiller. And by 1824 there were completed and published two encyclopedias, of twenty-one and forty-seven volumes respectively, that could have been produced nowhere else in the nation.

Penn's town yielded its pre-eminence slowly. As the center of business finance it was given the *coup de grâce* only in the 1830's, when Andrew Jackson scuttled Nicholas Biddle's Bank of the United States. By then, New York had become the nation's chief seaport and the "great commercial emporium" of the land. At the close of the War of 1812, England chose New York as the dumping ground for its accumulation of manufactures, a circumstance of which the alert merchants of Manhattan took immediate and full advantage. The early, precisely scheduled packet service to Europe that shuttled in and out of New York Harbor helped to concentrate transatlantic trade there, and the steamboats that proliferated on adjacent waters quickened the distribution of goods and people from everywhere. When the Erie Canal made New York the wideopen gateway to the West, no other city could challenge its status as the metropolis of the New World.

By then ideas that had been put into play at Philadelphia had, for almost a century, exercised a dynamic influence on the development of an American state of mind. Penn's great experiment of religious freedom had broadened into an experiment of every other sort of freedom—political, social, personal, and economic—upon which our national experience continues to pivot. By then, too, Philadelphia seemed ready to settle quietly back on its venerable reputation and, as a "hotbed of inertia," to become the butt of countless jokes (Philadelphians love to eat snails, but they find it so hard to catch them, etc.). Yet within the last dozen years, no other city has made such a remarkable effort to recover from the paralyzing blight that has afflicted our urban centers. The exact site of Penn's "green countrie towne" has been opened up and developed as the largest single space available at the center of an American city in the twentieth century; opened up into a vision of what a city can do for its own salvation. In this modern revolutionary stage of its history, Philadelphia has set the pace for urban America. But then, revolution and modernism are an old story in Philadelphia.

Marshall B. Davidson, a member of this magazine's Advisory Board, is Editor of Publications at New York's Metropolitan Museum of Art, author of Life in America, *and a contributor to* Romance of North America.

Further reading: Rebels and Gentlemen, *by Carl Bridenbaugh (Reynal, 1942);* Philadelphia, Holy Experiment, *by Struthers Burt (Doubleday, 1945);* Saga of American Society, *by Dixon Wecter (Scribner's, 1957).*

READING, WRITING, AND HISTORY

By BRUCE CATTON

Where the Buck Stops

When Harry Truman was President of the United States, he kept on his desk a little sign which announced: "The Buck Stops Here." This was his salty way of acknowledging the constitutional provision which makes the President the commander in chief of the country's armed forces and hence vests in him the terrible responsibility for making the life-or-death decisions that have to be made in time of crisis. Elaborate machinery has been set up to inform and guide the President, but the final answers still have to come from him. He can never pass the buck. It comes to the end of the line on his own blotter.

The founding fathers gave the President this power with some misgivings, sensing that this grant of authority was one of the key sections of the Constitution. The simple fact was that the responsibility had to be lodged somewhere. To divide it between Congress and President seemed clearly impractical, and to vest it in the legislature seemed, in the light of past experience, to risk putting too much power in the hands of a soldier. To give the power to the President seemed safest.

Things have changed since those days. The first "war President," James Madison, had an Army of a few thousand men, a Navy composed of a handful of cruisers and patrol craft, and a War Department whose entire personnel could have convened in one room. Today, by contrast, there are the immense Pentagon apparatus, the National Security Council, the Central Intelligence Agency, and all the rest—an almost incomprehensibly complex array of planners and doers.

But the authority remains undiluted. The President still has to say Yes or No. He can neither ignore nor delegate his power; he can only use it.

To see what American Presidents have done with this authority in times of war, Professor Ernest R. May of Harvard has assembled and edited a most enlightening book, *The Ultimate Decision,* in which a number of writers trace the growth and explore the significance of this charter of authority from 1812 to the present day, and in which Mr. May examines the profound underlying question: Has the job of commander in chief become too great, too complex, and too terrible a job for any one man?

Different war Presidents made their own contributions to the steady expansion of the scope of the Executive's war powers. Some, like McKinley, were reluctant to use these powers and proceeded with great caution;

The Ultimate Decision: the President as Commander in Chief, edited, with an introduction, by **Ernest R. May.** George Braziller Inc. 290 pp. $6.00.

---

others, like Lincoln, reached out unhesitatingly to use all of the authority they could get, setting precedents of far-reaching importance. But in the main all of them simply followed the rule the Constitution itself had laid down. As Marcus Cunliffe remarks in his perceptive chapter on Madison's experience: "In war, the President's powers grow almost despite himself." The game was set up that way, and that was the only way to play it.

Madison made this discovery about presidential powers: James K. Polk carried the discovery a step farther. Leonard D. White shows that in the Mexican War the President was given neither the information nor the legislative equipment to make full use of his authority, but he concludes that in spite of handicaps Polk did achieve a genuine unity of command. He proved, as Mr. White puts it, that "a President could also be a commander in chief. A President could run a war."

Lincoln is often accused of interfering too much in matters of strategy and tactics. T. Harry Williams points out that in doing this he was merely following the established American tradition which came out of the Revolutionary War, the War of 1812, and the Mexican War: "Lincoln was acting only as the civil authority had acted in every previous war. He was doing what he and most people thought the commander in chief ought to do in war."

In World War I, Wilson largely supported the decisions of his military men. Earlier, however, he had clearly shown the services who was boss. In 1913, when a quarrel with Japan produced a brief war scare, the Joint Board of the Army and Navy made certain recommendations about fleet movements in the Philippine area. Wilson rejected these recommendations, and the Joint Board protested and asked him to reconsider. Icily, Wilson told the Secretary of the Navy that when the President had finally adopted a policy, the admirals and generals could make no protests, "and I wish you would say to them that if this should occur again, there will be no General or Joint Boards. They will be abolished."

Perhaps we are still too close to Franklin Roosevelt and to Truman to reach even moderately objective appraisals of the way they exercised their war powers. Roosevelt is often accused of letting the military men run the show with too little direction by the civil power; Truman, whose climactic break with General Douglas MacArthur is a matter of very recent memory, is accused of interfering too much. Whatever the final verdict on these points may be, both men were aware of the extent of their powers and used them. Indeed, tracing the course of events in the Korean War, Wilber W. Hoare, Jr., concludes that "in more respects than most, Truman was the commander in chief envisioned by the writers of the Constitution."

Which brings us down to the present day—in which things are vastly different. Such Presidents as Lincoln, Wilson, and even Roosevelt could do without a great mass of technical and scientific knowledge; today's President cannot. He must distinguish, for instance, between kiloton and megaton weapons—the difference between which, as Mr. May remarks, "is roughly that between Bronx Park and Bronx County." He must

know a good deal about rocketry. He must have broad knowledge about the intricate military organizations that have been built up around these awesome weapons. He must know so much, indeed, that the question is often raised: Is the joint burden of the Presidency and the command-in-chief so great that it must be divided? If so, just how can the division be made? Do we go back to the system of the Roman republic and have, in effect, two consuls, a President and an almost equal deputy? Must our President, in future, be commander in chief in name only?

Mr. May thinks not. The basic decisions still have to be made by someone, and strategy must continue to remain the servant of policy. Whether they were right or wrong, wise or stupid, all of our Presidents who have waged war have done so as politicians, with a final sense of responsibility to public opinion. To Mr. May, it finally comes down to this: "The issue is not only whether one man can stand the double strain of the Presidency and the command-in-chief, but also whether the nation can stand to have any man except one, the President *and* commander in chief, determine what its fate shall be."

Failure of a President

One American President usually gets omitted from the list of chief executives who have led their countrymen in time of war. Jefferson Davis was also a war President; and if he was not President of the United States, he was at least President of an American nation whose constitution, as far as war powers were concerned, was almost identical with that of the United States. Is it possible to shed any light on the general question of how a President must act in time of war by examining his experience?

Davis was no man to let any scrap of presidential authority go unused. He was commander in chief, and he worked at it day and night, in season and out of season; his trouble, as a matter of fact, may have been that he worked at it too much, concerning himself with masses of detail that clerks might have handled and reducing his Secretary of War to a limited and subordinate position. But in any event, no one in the Confederacy was ever in the least doubt about who was running things.

The question, then, is how all of this worked out; and a sharply critical answer is returned by Clifford Dowdey in *Lee's Last Campaign*, which is of course principally a study of Robert E. Lee's actions during the final year of the Civil War but which also, of necessity, is an examination of Davis' actions as commander in chief.

Mr. Dowdey, studying the 1864 campaign in Virginia in great detail and with expert knowledge, concludes that General Lee was ruinously handicapped by President Davis' supervision. The chief trouble was not that the President told Lee when, where, and how to fight; Davis was much too intelligent to try anything like that, and Lee would not have stood for it if he had tried it. But Davis had set up a rigid, compartmentalized system for the control of the Confederacy's separate armies, and this system he refused to modify even when the enemy was at the gates. Not until it was too late was Lee able to exercise control over all of the forces that were resisting the Federal drive on Richmond. In effect, the Confederacy in its hour of supreme peril opposed a badly divided command to a command that had been grimly unified. The result was disaster.

General Ulysses S. Grant, supreme commander of the Federal forces, set out in May of 1864 to crush the Confederate armies in Virginia and take Richmond. His principal weapon was the powerful Army of the Potomac, which Grant led directly against Lee's Army of Northern Virginia. In addition, Grant had two other armies: one led by General Benjamin Butler, which came up the James River prepared to capture Petersburg, the railroad junction whose loss would involve the loss of Richmond; the other, General Franz Sigel's Army of the Shenandoah, which was to move up the great valley of Virginia, cut off the principal source of Lee's supplies, and eventually move east and come in on Richmond from the rear.

Against these, Lee could control only his own Army of Northern Virginia. The defense against Butler was out of his department, and he had nothing to do with it; similarly with the defense against Sigel. Luckily for

---

Lee's Last Campaign: the Story of Lee and His Men Against Grant, 1864, by Clifford Dowdey. Little, Brown and Co. 415 pp. $6.00.

Lee, both Butler and Sigel were generals of surpassing incompetence, who managed to fumble their assignments with an all-embracing woolliness of mind; the Federals failed to win an easy victory which two moderately skilled soldiers would have won without more than half an effort, and Lee was permitted to go on making his extremely skillful and devoted campaign against Grant's principal army. But the fundamental flaw in the Confederate defense system proved ruinous. Lee put up, against the Army of the Potomac, a defense which should have been effective; but because he could not control the armies which resisted the other prongs of Grant's offensive, this defense was practically nullified, and Lee was at last pinned within the lines at Petersburg, condemned to fight a war which he

could not hope to win. The Federal superiority in man power and material resources was allowed to exert its force. Once the siege of Petersburg began, the outcome—as Lee himself had foreseen from the beginning—was simply a matter of time.

This, according to Mr. Dowdey, was principally Davis' fault. He would not turn over supreme command of all the armies in Virginia to Lee—not until it was too late. He confined Lee to one small sector of the whole. In that sector Lee proved as effective as ever, but to be effective in this one area was not enough. The Federals were making an all-out push; Lee was condemned to make a limited reply, and despite his military genius a limited reply could not be good enough.

Davis was the constitutional commander in chief; he understood the exact scope of his powers, and he used them with courage and devotion. The real trouble, if Mr. Dowdey has it right—and it would be hard to quarrel with him very seriously—was that Davis used them in the wrong way.

An American President is responsible for everything his country does in time of war. He has been given extraordinary powers, and he is supposed to use them to win a victory. But that does not necessarily mean that he must exert constant, day-by-day control over the things his armies do. He controls high policy, which means that the victory which his armies win must at last be the kind of victory that will make his political aims secure, but he goes beyond that at his peril. Once he sees himself as primarily the strategist and the tactician, the man without whose consent no soldier may move, fire a musket, or button his coat, he begins to interfere with the experts who are supposed to be at his service but who must be allowed to achieve his aims in their own way.

The President, then, who is commander in chief, must understand and use his powers to the full, but he must not abuse them. Probably it is just as well that he usually is not a trained soldier himself; not being one, he is more likely to understand his own limitations. One of the fascinating aspects of the comparison between Davis and Lincoln is that Davis was a trained soldier and Lincoln was an unblemished amateur. Being a trained soldier, Davis tried to *be* a soldier, and the outcome was ruin for his cause. Being wholly untrained, Lincoln came before long to see that there were things he could not do, and so he let the soldiers do them. The result was victory.

Davis is a tragic and appealing figure in American history. He failed, mostly because the cards were stacked against him, but at least in part because he was too literal in his interpretation of the duties of the civilian commander in chief. Mr. Dowdey's book makes an ex-

cellent companion piece to the study engineered by
Mr. May.

The Meaning of Victory

Meanwhile, there was Lincoln, who—perhaps more than any other President—saw the full potentialities of a President's wartime powers and used them up to the hilt. What about him? What came of his essay in understanding and exercising the enormous authority which the Constitution gives to a chief executive in time of war?

A great deal came of it, including a complete transformation of American society and a revolutionary change in the American scheme of things. Lincoln accepted the challenge of secession in 1861 as something revolutionary, and he did not hesitate to use revolutionary means to meet it. His war powers, as he saw them, were all but unlimited; in effect, he believed that as commander in chief he could do just about anything that needed to be done to win the war, and most of these things he unhesitatingly did. America has never been the same since.

Allan Nevins looks into all of this in the sixth volume of his monumental examination of the causes, development, outcome, and effect of the Civil War, entitled *The War for the Union: War Becomes Revolution, 1862–1863*. He begins his story early in 1862, when the Federal cause seemed to be winning on all fronts, takes it through the disasters which were inflicted in the spring and summer of that year, and goes on to the beginning of the summer of 1863, when the Union cause was on the verge of winning the enormous victories of Vicksburg and Gettysburg; and he is concerned not so much with showing how and why an apparent victory turned to defeat and then became victory again, as with tracing what happened to the American nation in the process.

What happened to the nation, as Mr. Nevins sees it, was that in effect it was born anew. It became a different nation. It had been loose, amorphous, a sprawling agglomeration of people and resources which, amoeba-like, had no real central nervous system and no real sense of direction. It became hard, compact, organized, a modern America swinging enthusiastically into the industrial revolution, compressing into a few years a development which otherwise might have taken decades, or for that matter might have come out quite differently; and this happened, mostly, because the President with intense singleness of purpose marshaled all of the country's powers for victory in war.

To do all of this, Mr. Nevins believes, Lincoln had to handle a political-party revolution, an economic revolution, and a social revolution—and, possibly, an intellectual revolution as well. His armies not only had to win victories in the field; they had to be organized, equipped, transported, and supported in such a way that the victories would be possible, and to do all of this changed the nation. The American businessmen had to learn—and the war soon taught them—that they could "create a new economic world as the Revolutionary generation had created a new political world." The ordinary citizen had to learn that the great war for the Union had to become a war for human freedom as well if it were to be won; the politicians had to learn that their separate struggles for power and advantage must be keyed to the dominating fact of a North unified at least enough to bring its full power to bear on the rebellion; and the soldiers had to learn

---

The War for the Union: War Becomes Revolution, 1862–1863, by Allan Nevins. Charles Scribner's Sons. 557 pp. $7.50.

---

that their part was to win victories in the field, leaving it to the government at Washington to say just what those victories were aimed at.

All of this, with immense endurance and staggering effort, Lincoln brought about; and Mr. Nevins' point is that although Federal victory early in 1862 would simply have meant reunion, with no great change in the country that had gained reunion, victory postponed past Vicksburg and Gettysburg necessarily meant a fundamental change in the state of the American nation, the American economy, and American society. The effort that would have to be made after the spring of 1862 would be so profound that it would force changes whether anyone wanted them or did not want them. Once the war got past its mid-point, it was revolution, regardless of what anyone wanted.

How much of all of this did Lincoln himself see at the time? The question is impossible to answer definitely. Lincoln was in a position where he had to improvise, and what comes of improvisations when a nation's future is at stake is anyone's guess. The point is that he took the powers that had been given him and used them to the full—and always for a political purpose. His generals might do, or might want to do, this, that, or the other thing; Lincoln concerned himself all the time with what the victory they were fighting for would finally mean, and he never let anyone take the control of that aspect of the war away from him. Once he had found the technicians he needed—the Grants, Shermans, Thomases and so on—he gave them carte blanche. But he never allowed the central thread to get out of his hands.

All in all, these three books belong together.

Account of a Buyer of Bargains

I AM the husband of a buyer of bargains. My wife has somewhere heard, that a good houfewife never had any thing to purchafe, when it was wanted. This maxim is often in her mouth, and always in her head. She is not one of thofe philofophical talkers that fpeculate without practice, and learn fentences of wifdom only to repeat them; fhe never paffes by a fhop where furniture is fold, but fhe fpies fomething that *may be wanted fome time*, and it is impoffible to make her pafs the door of a houfe where fhe hears goods felling by auction.

Whatever fhe thinks cheap, fhe holds it the duty of an œconomift to purchafe; in confequence of this maxim, we are incumbered on every fide with ufelefs lumber. The fervants can fcarcely creep to their beds through the chefts and boxes that furround them. The carpenter is always employed in building clofets, fixing cupboards, and faftening fhelves; and my houfe has the appearance of a fhip ftored for a voyage acrofs the Atlantic.

I had often obferved that advertifements fet her on fire, and therefore, pretending to emulate her laudable frugality, I forbade the newfpaper to be taken any longer; but my precaution is vain; I know not by what fatality, or by what confederacy, every catalogue of *genuine furniture* comes to her hand, every advertifement of a warehoufe newly opened, is in her pocket-book; and fhe knows, before any of her neighbours, when the ftock of any man, leaving off trade, is to be fold *cheap for ready money*.

Such intelligence is to my *dear* one, the firen's fong. No engagement, no duty, no intereft, can with-hold her from a fale, from which fhe always returns congratulating herfelf upon her dexterity at a bargain; the porter lays down his burden in the hall, fhe difplays her new acquifitions, and fpends the reft of the day in contriving where they fhall be put.

As fhe cannot bear to have any thing incomplete, one purchafe neceffitates another; fhe has twenty feather-beds more than fhe can ufe, and lately another fale has fupplied her with a proportionable number of blankets, a large roll of linen for fheets, and five quilts for every bed, which fhe bought, becaufe the feller told her, that, if fhe would clear his hands, he would let her have a bargain.

Thus, by hourly encroachments, my habitation is made narrower and narrower; the dining-room is fo crouded with tables, that dinner fcarcely can be ferved; the parlour is decorated with fo many piles of china, that I dare not come within the door; at every turn of the ftairs, I have a clock, and half the windows of the upper floors are darkened, that fhelves may be fet before them.

This, however, might be borne, if fhe would gratify her own inclinations without oppofing mine. But though contrary to my tafte, fhe condemns me to live upon falt provifions. She knows the lofs of buying in fmall quantities: we have therefore whole hogs, and quarters of oxen; part of our meat is tainted before it is eaten, and part is thrown away, becaufe it is fpoiled; but fhe perfifts in her fyftem, and will never buy any thing by fingle pennyworths.

The common vice of thofe who are ftill grafping at more, is to neglect that which they already poffefs; but from this failing my wife is free. It is the great care of her life that the pieces of beef fhould be boiled in the order in which they are bought; that every feather-bed fhould be lain on in its turn; that the carpets fhould be taken out of the chefts once a month, and brufhed, and the rolls of linen opened now and then before the fire. She is daily enquiring after the beft traps for mice; and keeps the rooms always fcented by fumigations, to deftroy the moths. She employs workmen, from time to time, to adjuft fix clocks that never go, and clean five jacks that ruft in the garret; and a woman in the next alley, lives by fcouring the brafs and pewter, which, when fcoured, are only laid up again to tarnifh.

She is always imagining fome diftant time in which fhe fhall ufe whatever fhe accumulates: fhe has four looking-glaffes, which fhe cannot hang up in her houfe, but which will be handfome in more lofty rooms; and pays rent for the place of a vaft copper, in fome warehoufe, becaufe, when we live in the country, we fhall brew our own beer.

Of this life I have long been weary, but know not how to change it; all the married men, whom I confult, advife me to have patience; but fome old bachelors are of opinion, that, fince fhe loves fales fo well, fhe fhould have a fale of her own; and I have, I think, refolved to open her hoards, and advertife an auction.

From Mathew Carey's The American Museum, or Repository, *April, 1787; contributed by Mrs. Tally McKee of Pittsburgh.*